# Mountains

# [1001]

# [photos]

© 2008 Éditions Solar, an imprint of Place des Éditeurs
© 2009 Rebo International, b.v., Lisse, Netherlands

Text: Michel Viard
Graphic Design: Gwénaël Le Cossec
Editorial Coordinators: Gracieuse Licari and Olivier Pillé
Printing: Frédéric Bar
Translation: Matthew Clarke for First Edition Translations Ltd, Cambridge, UK
Editor: Wendy Toole for First Edition Translations Ltd
Typesetting: Garamond Studio, Prague, Czech republic
Copy Editor: Elizabeth A. Haas

ISBN: 978 90 366 2510 4

# Mountains
# [1001]
# [photos]

REBO
PUBLISHERS

# Contents

# Mountains
of Europe

**N**orway is the most mountainous of the Scandinavian countries. The very word Scandinavia comes from *scande*, which means "mountain range." Here, Sami people can still be seen amid spectacular landscapes, leading their herds of reindeer from the valleys to the high mountain pastures.

Norway is sliced in half by a mountain range over 995 mi. (1,600 km) long. It comprises gigantic glaciers, such as those in the hinterland of Bergen, where magnificent fjords are bounded by vertical granite walls. The peaks are not particularly high, but as the altitude at the bottom of the valleys is so low, the slopes often plunge down for over 3,280 ft. (1,000 m). The highest peak in the Scandinavian Alps is Galdhøpiggen, at 8,100 ft. (2,469 m), followed by Glittertind at 8,087 ft. (2,465 m). These two peaks have long been considered the highest in Norway, but Glittertind is covered with ice that is inexorably melting as a result of global warming.

These two mountains are within the reach of fit hikers but this is not true of the lower summits, such as the Store Trolltind, at 5,866 ft. (1,788 m); the Trollryggen, at 5,715 ft. (1,742 m); and, especially, the Trollveggen ("Wall of Trolls"), one of the holy grails of mountain climbers. Its vertical faces pose a daunting challenge, especially in winter, when they turn into sheets of ice. Elsewhere, superb facilities have been installed to allow hikers to enjoy magnificent mountain scenery in numerous parks, particularly the Jotunheimen National Park, which is spread over 250,000 acres dotted with mountains

# Scandinavian Mountain Ranges

including Børgefjell, which culminates 5,587 ft. (1,703 m) above the River Vefsna. Footpaths wind through the valleys and around lakes and waterfalls, before weaving their way up sixty glaciers to some of Norway's highest peaks.

[1] The village of Gudvangen, in western Norway, is situated at the end of the Nærøy Fjord, which is some 12 mi. (20 km) long. The fjord was declared a UNESCO World Heritage Site in 2005.
[2] The village of Fjærland, in the Norwegian county of Sogn og Fjordane, has a glacier museum.
[3] and [6] The Geiranger Fjord, also listed as a UNESCO World Heritage Site since 2005, is situated to the south of the Norwegian county of Møre og Ramsdal. The village of Geiranger, at the far end of the fjord, has a port that can accommodate seagoing ships.
[4] Lofoten Islands, Norway.
[5] Reflections in the still waters of the Fjærland Fjord.

[1] Lofoten Islands, Norway.
[2] Historic Icelandic farmhouses covered with peat.
[3] Climbing the Nigards Glacier in the Jostedal National Park, in southwest Norway.
[4] Taking a breather at the foot of the spectacular Briksdal Glacier in Norway. It can be reached from Olden, a town situated at the northern end of Nordfjord.
[5] Sarek National Park in Swedish Lapland, seen here in the fall.
[6] Mount Pierikpakte, in the Sarek National Park, Sweden.

[1] The Sognefjord, the longest fjord in Europe, thrusts forward for 127 mi. (204 km), with an average width of 2.8 mi. (4.5 km), making it also the widest fjord in Norway. At some points it is over 4,265 ft. (1,300 m) deep.

[2] Glaciers overlooking the village of Stryn, situated near the end of the Nordfjord in Norway.

[3] Fjord in the county of Sogn og Fjordane, in western Norway.
[4] Briksdal Glacier, in Norway's Jostedal National Park.
[5] Jostedal Glacier, Norway.

[1] Village of Flåm, tucked into the tip of a Norwegian valley.
[2] The port of Balestrand in the Sognefjord, on the southwest coast of Norway.

[Opposite page]
The imposing Preikestolen ("Pulpit Rock"), near Stavanger, in southern Norway, looms over the Lysefjord, which receives 80,000 tourists every year.

[1] Midnight sun on the island of Senja, in the Andfjord, Norway.
[2] Farms and fields in the county of Sogn og Fjordane, in western Norway.
[3] The banks of the Sognefjord, in Norway.

[4] The typical Danish-style port of Uummannaq, Greenland.
[5] The church of Snæfellsnes-og Hnappadalssysla, Iceland.

[1] The Norwegian Coastal Express (Hurtigruten) crosses the Arctic Circle between Bergen and Kirkenes.
[2] Port of Ballstad, in Norway.
[3] Island of Vestvagoy.
[4] Climbing the Briksdal Glacier in Norway.

[5] The Pulpit Rock in southern Norway soars to 1,982 ft. (604 m) above the Lysefjord.
[6] The Lyngenfjord, in Norway.
[7] The Hardangerfjord, situated to the east of Bergen, in Norway, stretches 113 mi. (183 km) inland.
[8] Waterfall plunging into Lake Loenvatnet.

**2**

[1] Plateau in Swedish Lapland.
[2] Midnight sun reflected on the waters of Lake Kilpisjärvi, in the northwest tip of Finland, the country's most mountainous region.
[3] Climbing Mount Åreskutan in Sweden.

[Right] Padjelanta National Park, a UNESCO World Heritage Site in northern Sweden.

The Alps form a mountain range 750 mi. (1,200 km) long and 190–250 mi. (300–400 km) wide. Stretching from southern Germany through Slovenia, Liechtenstein, Switzerland, France, and Italy, they boast over eighty peaks higher than 13,000 ft. (4,000 m).

The Alps provide Europe with its ceiling: Mont Blanc, which soars to a height of 15,780 ft. (4,810 m). This giant is surrounded by twenty-six other peaks of over 12,000 ft. (4,000 m), such as the Grandes Jorasses, which culminate at Walker's Point (13,800 ft./4,206 m), followed by the peaks of Margherita, Elena, Croz, and Whymper. Further on, the Giant's Tooth rises to 13,169 ft. (4,014 m), while the massif of the Oisans, complete with some fifty glaciers, stands between the valleys of the Rhone and Italy. These magnificent peaks form part of the Parc National des Écrins (occupying more than 340 sq. mi. (880 km2), where the bearded lammergeyer has just been reintroduced and wolves have started to appear again, wandering in from Italy.

Straddling Switzerland and Italy, the famous granite pyramid of the Matterhorn rises to 14,678 ft. (4,474 m), while Monte Rosa is the highest peak in Switzerland at 15,203 ft. (4,634 m). The impressive massif near Bern is dominated by three peaks: the Jungfrau ("Virgin," 13,642 ft./4,158 m); the Mönch ("Monk," 13,448 ft./4,099 m) and the Eiger ("Bear," 13,025 ft./3,970 m). The Eiger has gained notoriety all over the world as it is very dangerous to climb and has claimed numerous victims. One of the most beautiful ice mountains in the Alps is located in Italy, between Lombardy and the Tyrol: Ortles (12,812 ft./3,905 m). This grand peak is home to the lynx, as well as the friendly yaks that graze nearby the museum devoted to the mountain.

# The Alps and the Pre-Alps

The highest mountain in Austria is the Grossglöckner (12,461 ft./3,798 m), set in the Hohe Tauern National Park, which is spread over 440 acres, making it the largest protected area in the Alps. In Slovenia—the only country to display an image of a mountain on its national flag—the Alps are dominated by Mount Triglav, at 9,396 ft. (2,864 m).

[1] The Needles of Chamonix are rugged peaks in the Mont Blanc massif, in the French Alps.

[2] The snow on the French side of Mont Blanc reveals the remains of a trail.

[3] Climbers tackling a crevasse on Mont Blanc du Tacul (13.937 ft./4,248 m), one of the peaks in the Mont Blanc massif.

[4] The Aiguille du Midi cable car crosses the White Valley from Chamonix in Haute-Savoie.

[5] A climber on top of the Aiguillette d'Argentière contemplates the Chamonix Valley in the French Alps. The Aiguille du Chardonnet can be seen in the background.

[6] The Black Lake, in the heart of the Red Needles massif in Haute-Savoie, lies at an altitude of 8,530 ft. (2,600 m).

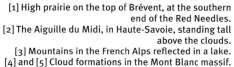

[1] High prairie on the top of Brévent, at the southern end of the Red Needles.
[2] The Aiguille du Midi, in Haute-Savoie, standing tall above the clouds.
[3] Mountains in the French Alps reflected in a lake.
[4] and [5] Cloud formations in the Mont Blanc massif.

[1] and [2] A roped party of climbers scaling Mont Blanc, in the French Alps.
[3] Glaciers in the Mont Blanc massif, in Haute-Savoie.

[4] Mountains in the French Alps.
[5] The glaciers of La Grivola and the Grand Paradis massif.

31

[1] The Meije massif looming over Lake Lérié, situated at a height of 8,038 ft. (2,450 m) in the Hautes-Alpes.
[2] Lake Roselend, in Savoie, is constrained by a dam. To the rear, the Roc du Vent (7,743 ft./2,360 m).
[3] La Clusaz, situated at the foot of the Aravis massif in Haute-Savoie.
[4] View of the southern Alps from Mount Ventoux.
[5] Mount Ventoux, popularly known as the "Giant of Provence," is the highest mountain in the Vaucluse.

[1] The Dentelles de Montmirail overlooking the village of Sablet. [2] The village of Roussillon, with Mount Ventoux in the background.

[Right] The snow-capped peak of Mount Ventoux dominates the village of Brante.

[1] Lake Basto, in the Mercantour National Park.
[2] and [4] The Vallée des Merveilles, in the Mercantour National Park.

[3] **Mercantour National Park.**

[1] French Alpine mountains seen from Digne.
[2] Sunset on the Vercors massif.
[3] The Grande Chartreuse Monastery,
famous for its liqueurs.

[4] Mount Aiguille in the Vercors massif.
[5] Vercors National Park in the French Alps.

39

[1] View of the Vercors National Park from the top of Mount Jocou, in the Pre-Alps, on the border between the Isère and the Drôme.
[2] Mount Aiguille, to the south of the Isère, forms part of the western escarpment of the Vercors massif.
[3] At 7,680 ft. (2,341 m), the Grand Veymont is the culminating point of the Vercors massif.

[4 to 6] Mount Cervin, on the Italian-Swiss frontier, is also known as the Matterhorn. It is 14,692 ft. (4,478 m) high. On the Swiss side, it towers over Lake Grindji and the village of Findeln.

41

[1] The Aletsch glacier, in the Bern region of the Swiss Alps.
[2] The Eiger, famous for its North Face, overlooks the lush valley of Grindelwald in Switzerland.
[3] Alpine mountains in the Bern region of Switzerland.

[Right] Terraced vineyards by the village of Saint-Saphorin, on the Swiss bank of Lake Geneva.

[1] and [3] The legendary Matterhorn (or Mount Cervin) is considered the most beautiful of all Alpine mountains, on account of its pyramidal shape.
[2] In the height of the winter in 1993, Catherine Destivelle climbed the Matterhorn via the Bonatti route on the North Face.

[4] Along with the Aletsch glacier and the Bietschhorn, the Jungfrau (literally the "Young Woman") forms part of a UNESCO World Heritage Site.
[5] The Matterhorn, in southwest Switzerland.

[Following pages] Spiez with its castle, on the south bank of Lake Thoune, situated in the Oberland in Switzerland's Bern region.

[1] Zoppè di Cadore, Mount Pelmo (10,394 ft./3,168 m), in the Dolomites, Italy.
[2] The Three Peaks of Lavaredo, in Sesto National Park, Italy. The highest soars to 9,389 ft. (2,999 m).
[3] Sassolungo (10, 436 ft./3,181 m) and Sassopiatto (9,741 ft./2,969 m) in the Dolomites, in Italy.
[4] The Piz Boe refuge, in Italy.

[5] The small town of Tarvisio, not far from the Slovenian border in northeast Italy, is set on top of Mount Lussari (5,873 ft./1,790 m). It is famous for its 16th-century monastery, the Mount Lussari Sanctuary.
[6] The Ortles massif is named after its highest peak, which rises to 12,812 ft.(3,905) m on the Italian–Swiss frontier.

49

The upheaval that gave rise to the Alps in the Secondary Era also triggered the formation of the Jura, a pleated massif stretching in a crescent shape from the Rhone to the Rhine. Its very name is derived from the Jurassic Period of the Secondary Era, a time when the region was a warm sea.

The Alpine upsurge pushed up sediments and transformed this sea into mountains. The Jura comprises mountains in a roughly parallel formation, separated by valleys and sliced by chasms. The Jura mountain range culminates at 5,643 ft. (1,720 m) with the Crêt de la Neige. The other main peaks are the Crêt du Nu (4,314 ft./1,315 m), the Grand Colombier (5,023 ft./1,531 m), the Dent du Chat or "Cat's Tooth" (4,560 ft./1,390 m), which overlooks Lake Bourget, and Mount Tendre (5,509 ft./1,679 m).

The massif of the Vosges emerged in the Tertiary Era as Rhineland shifted downward, creating a gigantic fault.

The upsurge of the edges of this fault gave birth to two ranges on either side: the Upper Vosges and the Lower Vosges, a stunning array of reds, grays, and violets. The highest peak is found in the Upper Vosges: the Grand Ballon ("Big Ball"), also known as the Ballon de Guebwiller, at 4,672 ft. (1,424 m). Near it stands the Storkenkopf ("Stork's Head"), at 4,482 ft. (1,366 m). These peaks can be observed by hiking through the Col ("Pass") du Bonhomme and the Col de la Schlucht, along the Route of the Crests, which was created during World War I. The third highest mountain in the Vosges, the Hohneck (4,472 ft./ 1,363 m), separates Alsace from Lorraine and is also visible from this route, while the fourth highest, the Kastelberg (4,429 ft./

# The Jura and the Vosges

1,350 m), divides the French departments of the Haut-Rhin and Les Vosges. This is followed by the Klintzkopf (4,364 ft./1,330 m), home to a nature reserve, and the Rothenbachkopf (4,318 ft./1,316 m). As their name suggests, the Lower Vosges consist of smaller mountains, the highest being Mount Donon (3,310 ft./1,009 m).

[1] Vineyard at the foot of the Chalon Château, in the Jura.
[2] The rugged cirque, or corrie, of the Creux-du-Van, known as the "Swiss Grand Canyon."
[3] Lake Bourget.

[4] The town of Besançon, in Franche-Comté.
[5] Meadows and fir forests in the Swiss Jura.

[1] The mountain stage between Leukerbad and La Chaux-de-Fonds is one of the highlights of the Tour de Suisse cycling race.
[2] Snow-topped mountains in Alsace.

[Opposite page] Aerial view of the Swiss mountains.

[1] Villages of Kientzheim and Ammerschwihr, in Alsace.
[2] Valley of Sainte-Marie-aux-Mines, in Alsace.
[3 and right] Natural Park of the Vosges, in the territory of Belfort.

**T**he Massif Central dates back 500 million years, making it the oldest group of mountains in France. It is also the most extensive, as it covers an area of 32,800 sq. mi. (85,000 km²) in the middle of France. It also holds the distinction of containing the majority of the country's volcanoes.

Nowadays, all these volcanoes—over a thousand in total—are inactive. The first eruptions took place 25 million years ago, although the most intense period of activity occurred between 3 and 13 million years ago, when the Cantal, the Cézallier, and the Monts Dore appeared. Other volcanoes would emerge later—for example, those of the Puys range, which came into being recently, in geological terms, some 150,000 years ago. The youngest volcanoes in the Massif Central are the Puy de la Vache and Puy de Lassolas, both 8,500 years old, and the one forming the lake of the Pavin Crater, which is a mere 7,000 years old.

Not all these volcanoes are extinct; some are simply dormant may come to life again in around 3,000 years time. The erosion resulting from their venerable age has molded the tops of the Massif Central into rounded domes rather than spiky peaks. Its highest mountain is the Puy de Sancy (6,188 ft./1,886 m), a volcano that has ceased all activity but conceals springs replete with minerals and gases, particularly in Chaudefour and La Bourboule. The second highest mountain in the Massif Central is the Puy de Dôme (6,086 ft./1,855 m), the remains of Europe's biggest volcano, which, when active, must have soared to a height of over 9,850 ft. (3,000 m) and possessed a crater with a circumference of over 38 mi. (60 km). The Puy Mary, 5,850 ft.(1,783 m) high, is renowned for panoramic views of: the Valleys of La Santoire, La Petite Rue, Le Mars, La Maronne, L'Aspre, La Bertrande, and La Jordanne.

# The Massif Central

Other well-known mountains in the Massif Central include Mount Aigoual (5,142 feet/1,567 m), which forms part of the watershed between the Atlantic and the Mediterranean, and Mount Gerbier-de-Jonc (5,089 ft./1,551 m), which contains the source of the Loire.

[1] The glacial valley of the Fontaine Salée, in the Puy-de-Dome.
[2] The Puys mountain range, in the Puy-de-Dôme.
[3] The Regional Natural Park of the Volcanoes of Auvergne. In the background, the volcano that gives its name to an entire province, the Puy de Dôme, culminates at 4,810 ft. (1,466 m). It stands out from its neighbors on account of the radio mast on its summit.
[4] The gorges of the Tarn and the village of La Malène in Lozère.
[5] Département of the Puy-de-Dôme.
[6] The Cévennes region.
[7] Autumnal landscape near Issoire, in the Puy-de-Dôme.

[1] The Cévennes National Park, in Lozère.
[2] Small valley in the Aigoual massif, in the Cévennes region.
[3] The village of Saint-Cirq-Lapopie, in the Regional Natural Park of the Causses du Quercy, is tucked into an escarpment, 330 ft. (100 m) above the Lot.

[Right] The internationally famous village of Rocamadour is set in the Regional Natural Park of the Causses du Quercy, in the *département* of Le Lot, at the northern end of the Midi-Pyrénées region.

[1] The fortress of Polignac, near the Puy-en-Velay.
[2] The Solutré Rock in Burgundy won fame for being visited every year by François Mitterand.

[3] Hiking in the Regional Park of the Volcanoes of Auvergne.
[4] Sainte-Énimie overlooks the gorges of the Tarn.

[1] This balloon race forms part of the festival of La Bourboule.
[2] Mount Lozère looming over a Tarn valley shrouded in fog.

[Left] Rock covered with lichen on Mount Lozère, in Auvergne.

This long, thin chain of mountains stretches from the Atlantic to the Mediterranean. The Pyrenees, the oldest of all the Mediterranean Tertiary pleats, form a natural barrier, 270 mi. (435 km) long, between France and Spain.

This natural barrier comprises seventeen massifs: those of the Albères, the Arbailles, the Arize, the Besiberri, the Canigou, the Carlit, the Corbières, the Larra-Belagua, the Luchonnais, the Maladeta, the Mont-Perdu, the Montcalm, the Néouvielle, the Plantaurel, the Posets, the Tabe, and the Vignemale. Aneto (11,168 ft./3,404 m), on the Spanish side, is the highest mountain in the Pyrenees. The Pico de Posets (11,073 ft./3,375 m) and Monte Perdido (11,007 ft./3,355 m) are also situated in Spain. The next highest mountains are found on the French side, in the central Pyrenees: Vignemale (10,820 ft./3,298 m), the Pic de Perdiguère (10,571 ft./3,222 m), the Pic Long (10,472 ft./3,192 m), and the Pic Schrader (10,413 ft./3174 m).

These are set amid an array of lower mountains, some of which have managed to stand out from the crowd, whether by resembling a tooth, as in the case of the Pic du Midi d'Ossau (9,462 ft./2,884 m), or by playing host to an astronomical observatory, as does the Pic du Midi de Bigorre (9,423 ft./2,872 m). The Tour de France cycling race has bestowed fame on other Pyrenean mountains, including Aubisque (5,607 ft./1,709 m), Tourmalet (6,939 ft./2,115 m), and Aspin (4,885 ft./1,489 m).

The Pyrenees boast exceptional wildlife including some endemic species, such as the

# The Pyrenees and the Cantabrian Mountains

extremely rare Pyrenean desman, a small insectivore that was only discovered in 1811. Furthermore, bears have been reintroduced, sparking fierce debate among locals, shepherds, and ecologists; in contrast, the reintroduction of vultures—wild, black, and Egyptian—has been universally welcomed.

[1] A view of the Cirque de Gavarnie, in the Pyrenees National Park, which was classified as a UNESCO World Heritage Site in 1997.
[2] Mountains in the Hautes-Pyrénées, near Arreau, in France.
[3] and [4] Lush countryside in the French Basque country.
[5] A view of the Pyreneees from Bagnères-de-Bigorre (Hautes-Pyrénées, France).

[6] The Basque country covers an area of 7,935 sq. mi. (20,551 km²), divided between Spain and southwest France.

[7] The Cirque de Gavarnie, one of the most popularly visited sites in the Pyrenees, is made up of three successive stories that rise to a height of almost 4,921 ft. (1,500 m). Its diameter measures around 3.75 mi. (6 km).

[8] In the Ossau Valley, in the Pyrénées-Atlantiques, the Pic du Midi is easily distinguished by its shape, reminiscent of a tooth. It is 9,462 ft. (2,884 m) high, making it visible from the plains of Aquitaine.

[1] The Cerdagne, a pit resulting from subsidence, measures 419 sq. mi. (1,086 km²). It is divided almost equally between France and Spain.
[2] The Pyrenees seen from Catalonia, in Spain.
[3] The Cavall Bernat, one of the highest peaks in Montserrat, Spain.
[4] Montserrat means the "sawtooth mountain" in Catalan.

[5] The Colomina refuge in Catalonia.
[6] The Sierra del Cad, in the Natural Park of Cadí-Moixero, in Spain.
[7] North face of the Sierra del Cadí.

[1] and [4] The Anisclo Canyon in Spain's Ordesa National Park, is a gash in the southern side of Mont-Perdu.
[2] The River Arazas runs through the Ordesa Valley, in the Spanish Pyrenees.
[3] The village of Bestué is dominated by the imposing Mont-Perdu, in the Ordesa National Park, in Spain.

[5] The Green Valley in Spain's Ordesa National Park is overlooked by plunging escarpments.
[6] The Ainsa, in Spain.
[7] Mont-Perdu looms over the Green Valley in Spain.
[8] The Plana Canal and the Pena de l'Ombre in the Ordesa National Park, in Spain.

[1] A road winding through the Spanish Pyrenees.
[2] Ruins of the Quéribus Château in the Aude, France.
[3] Rocky slopes in the Albarracín massif, in Castile, Spain.

[Opposite page] La Morella, in Spain.

[1] Pico de Europa in Asturias, Spain.
[2] Lake Ercina, in Spain.
[3] A view of Corníon, in the Picos de Europa National Park.

[4] Picos de Europa National Park, in Spain.
[5] and [6] Pico de Europa.
[7] The Cares Gorge runs through the massif of the Picos de Europa.

79

The Apennines extend for over 600 mi. (1,000 km) from northern Italy to Sicily. This range is divided into three sections: the northern Apennines, a prolongation of the southern Alps; the central Apennines, which include the Abruzzo; and the southern Apennines, complete with Mount Etna and Mount Vesuvius.

The peaks in the northern Apennines do not exceed 6,000 ft. (2,000 m) in height, apart from Mount Cimone in the Tuscan-Emilian section, which rises to 7,103 ft. (2,165 m). The Abruzzos are higher, with nine mountains above 6,000 ft. (2,000 m) including the highest of all the Apennines, Como Grande, at 9,554 ft. (2,912 m). The southern Apennines are lower and more rounded, but they are particularly noteworthy for containing the only two active volcanoes remaining in the Mediterranean.

Etna, also the highest volcano in the Mediterranean, has been active for 600,000 years and erupts every twenty years or so—the most recent period ended in May 2007, after streams of lava had poured down into the sea and "bombs" of incandescent stone had hurtled out of the crater. Etna contains several craters, the highest of which currently reaches 10,892 ft. (3,320 m). During its quiet periods, hikers can take guided tours right up to the edge of these craters.

Vesuvius, in contrast, is not a particularly steep volcano (4,203 ft./1,281 m) and is dormant, not having erupted since 1944. It is, however, considered one of the most dangerous volcanoes in the world, as the magma in its crater generates huge explosions that propel ashes and thousands of rocks for dozens of miles. Vesuvius was responsible

# The Apennines

for the destruction of the Roman cities of Pompeii, Herculaneum, Oplontis, and Stabia, when it engulfed them under a deluge of ash on August 24, 79 AD. Not far away, another volcano with several craters, the Phlegrean Fields, still shows faint signs of activity in the form of wispy smoke, and is kept under close observation.

[1] Mount Etna, in Sicily.
[2] Eruption of lava on Etna.
[3] View of the Giardini Naxos Bay, in Sicily.
[4] Etna emitting smoke.
[5] and [6] The slopes of Etna after an eruption.
[7] Etna covered with snow in winter.

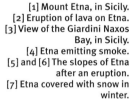

[Left] View of Mount Etna covered in snow,
as seen from the village of Randazzo.
[1 to 4] Etna showed signs of life in July 2005, prompting a state of
emergency in Sicily. For twenty days it spewed out tons of lava, and
only completely calmed down in May 2007.

[1 to 4] Etna is the most active volcano in Europe. Its crater spans an area of 11.5 sq. mi. (30 km²).

[5] and [6] The ejection of burning lava is an extraordinary sight, especially at night. [7] Etna emits smoke constantly, even in periods of repose.

87

[1] Vesuvius is now a dormant volcano.
[2] The ruins of Pompeii, with Vesuvius in the background.

[3] The Bay of Naples, with Vesuvius to the rear.
[4 to 7] Vesuvius looms over the Bay of Naples and is visible from a great distance.
[Following pages]
Naples, in the shadow of Vesuvius.

The word Balkans means "wooded mountain range" in Turkish. This group of mountains is located between the Black Sea to the east, the Adriatic and Ionian seas to the west, and the Aegean Sea to the south. The area is considered to be the site of the legendary city of Atlantis.

The origins of the myth of Atlantis can be traced back to the Santorini volcano, situated underneath the islands that comprise the Cyclades. It erupted around 1645 bc, destroying the island of Atlantis, the cradle of a Minoan civilization dating from the Bronze Age. The volcano later erupted on several other occasions—most recently in 1950—giving rise to a host of small islands. The entire region has suffered frequent earthquakes because of the significant activity of underwater volcanoes such as Kolumbo.

Mainland Greece is crossed by the Olympian Mountains. Their highest peak is Mytikas (9,570 ft./2,917 m), which is endowed with impressive limestone walls. It is flanked by Skòlio (9,550 ft./2,911 m), Stefâni (9,544 ft./2,909 m), and Skala (9,403 ft./2,866 m). The name of Mount Olympus itself means "very bright," and refers to the dazzling gleam of its summits in winter. It was in these mountains that Zeus established his earthly home after chasing out the Titans.

The highest mountain in the Balkan Mountains is in Bulgaria: Mount Musala (9,596 ft./2,925 m), its name meaning the "way of the Gods." Bulgaria is blessed with some extremely beautiful mountains, such as Mount Botev (7,795 ft./2,376 m), which is surrounded by the Djendem Nature Reserve and harbors one of the highest and most spectacular waterfalls in Europe. Mount Persenk (4,757 ft./1,450 m) is known for its "wonderful bridges," the result of water eroding the

# The Balkans

rock to create magnificent arches. Another famous mountain, Mount Shipka, stands as a symbol of Bulgarian resistance against the Ottoman Empire in 1878. Many of Bulgaria's most beautiful mountains, including Musala, are located within the country's extensive network of natural parks.

[1] Mountains surrounding the village of Kranj, in Slovenia.
[2] The River Soca, in Slovenia, is famous for its trout.

[3] The Vodnikov massif in the Triglav National Park, in Slovenia.
[4] Lake Bohini, in the Triglav National Park, in Slovenia.
[5] Lake Cernika, in Slovenia.

[1] and [2] Views of the Trenta Valley, in Slovenia.
[3] The village of Sorica, dominated by Mount Lajnar.
[4] The High Tatras, a massif in the Slovenian Carpathians.

[5] The River Cetina, in Croatia.
[6] Tulove Grede, in the Croatian Carpathians.
[7] View of the fortified town of Korcula, in Croatia.
[8] Sunset over Makarska, in Croatia.

[1] The Serbian Carpathians, seen from Sarajevo.
[2] The village of Drazin, on the Adriatic coast.
[3] Kotor Bay, on the Adriatic.
[4] Lake Jezero, in Croatia.

[5] Church on an island in Kotor Bay.
[6] Valley of the River Moraca.
[7] Mountain lake in Rila National Park, in Bulgaria.

[1] Mountains overlooking Tirana, in Albania.
[2] The Fierze Dam, in Albania.

[3] The foothills of the Santorini volcano.
[4] The Santorini volcano is connected with the story of the mysterious city of Atlantis.
[5] The town of Fira, situated on the crater of the Santorini volcano.
[6] The town of Thera, built on the slopes of an extinct volcano.
[Following pages] View of the Bay of Thera, in Greece.

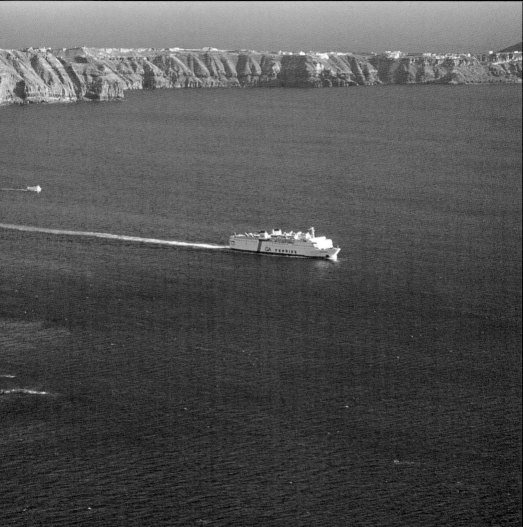

Villages tucked into
a valley overshadowed
by the Tatras massif, in Poland.

This mountain range forms part of the same arc as the Alps and the Balkans. The Carpathians are spread over several countries in Central and Eastern Europe: Slovakia, the Czech Republic, Poland, Romania, Serbia, the Ukraine, and Austria.

Geologists think that the Carpathians were formed as a result of alluvia originating from the Alps 6 million years ago, when the latter soared to heights of over 20,000 ft. (6,000 m). Their highest peak is Gerlachovsky in Slovakia on Mount Gerlach (8,711 ft./2,655 m). This is closely followed by Mount Moldoveanu (8,346 ft./2,544 m) in Romania and Mount Rysy (8,199 ft./2,499 m) in Poland.

The Carpathians, which span a circular arc measuring over 930 mi. (1,500 km) are divided into eight massifs: the Outer Western Carpathians, the Inner Western Carpathians, the Outer Eastern Carpathians, the Inner Eastern Carpathians, the Southern Carpathians, the Romanian Western Carpathians, the Transylvanian Plateau, and the Serbian Carpathians. In contrast to the Alps, the Carpathian massifs are fairly dispersed, because of the numerous valleys that divide them into segments. The peaks are less pointed than those of the Alps and considerably lower. The highest massifs are found in Romania: the Rodna Mountains (7,556 ft./2,303 m), surrounded by lakes and deep caves; the Rodnei Mountains, crowned by the Pietrosul (7,562 ft./2,305 m); and the Bucegi massif, with the Omu (8,218 ft./2,505 m), Bucara (8,212 ft./2,503 m), Bucsoiu (8,176 ft./2,492 m), and Costila (8,169 ft./2,490 m).

The Fagaras massif culminates at 8,343 ft. (2,543 m) with Mount Moldoveanu. The Retezat massif reaches 8,232 ft. (2,509 m) with the Peleaga, while that of Piatra Craiului

# The Carpathians

reaches 7,346 ft. (2,239 m) with Omu. In all, these Romanian Carpathians contain 300 peaks over 6,000 ft. (2,000 m) high and thirteen peaks over 7,500 ft. (2,500 m) high, but elsewhere this range rarely exceeds 5,905 ft. (800 m).

[1] The peak of Dumbier (6,703 ft./2,043 m) in the Tatras massif.
[2] The Tatras massif, in Slovakia.

[3] The Tatras massif seen from Poprad, in Slovakia.
[4] and [5] The Tatras massif.
[6] Popradské Pleso, in the Tatras massif.

[1] The Romanian city of Brasov, often called "the jewel of the Carpathians."
[2] The Piatra Craiului culminates at 7,346 ft. (2,239 m) with Omu.

[3] Moeciu de Jos, in Romania.
[4] Climbers on the upper
reaches of the Tatras massif.
[5] A village in the valley below
the Tatras massif.

Mountains
of Asia

Everest, the roof of the world,
soars to 29,029 ft. (8,848 m)
behind the peaks of Lhotse
and Nuptse.

The Himalayas, which run through Pakistan, Nepal, China, Tibet, and India for over 1,250 mi. (2,000 km), comprise the world's fifty highest mountains, and all of its fourteen peaks of 24,000 ft. (8,000 m) plus. The highest, at 29,029 ft. (8,848 m), is Everest, the roof of the world.

The highest mountain in the world, which stands within the boundaries of Nepal and Tibet, owes its name to George Everest, the Welsh geographer who first identified and measured it. It was not until 1953 that the New Zealander Edmund Hillary and the Sherpa Tenzing Norgay conquered its peak. Many climbers have made it to the top since then: over 500 achieved this feat in 2006. The world's second highest mountain is K2, officially measured at 28,251 ft. (8,611 m) despite recent claims of a total of 28,268 ft. (8,616 m high); the ascent of this mountain is situated between India and China is considered by climbers to be the most difficult of all, and only 300 have managed it.

In third place comes Kangchenjunga (28,169 ft./8,586 m), which stands alongside Makalu (27,766 ft./8,463 m), the fifth in the list of the 24,000 ft. (8,000 m) plus. The world's fourth highest mountain is Lhotse (27,940 ft./8,516 m), which has Lhotse Shar (27,552 ft./8,398 m) as its neighbor. These are followed by Cho Oyu (26,906 ft./8,201 m), Dhaulagiri (26,795 ft./8,167 m), Manaslu (26,781 ft./8,163 m), Nanga Parbat (26,660 ft./8,126 m), and Annapurna (26,545 ft./8,091 m), first climbed by the Frenchman Maurice Herzog. Gasherbrum (26,470 ft./8,068 m), surrounded by six peaks over 27,966 ft. (7,000 m) high, takes eleventh place in the table of the 24,000 ft. (8,000 m) plus, which is completed by the Broad Peak

# The Himalayas

(26,401 ft./8,047 m), Gasherbrum II (26,361 ft./8,035 m), and finally Shishapangma (26,335 ft./8,027 m).

All these peaks have now been conquered, but at the price of the lives of over 6,000 climbers—a figure that goes up every year, as these mountains still present an extremely daunting challenge.

[1] Ama Dablam (22,493 ft./6,856 m) and Lhotse (27,940 ft./8,516 m).
[2] Panoramic view from Syangboche (12,566 ft./3,830 m), in the Sagamartha National Park.
[3] Khumbu Valley in Nepal, the base camp for the ascent of Everest.
[4] Avalanche on Pumori.
[5] The peaks of Everest and Nuptse.
[6] Lake Gokyo, in Nepal.

[1] Glacier on Everest.
[2] Crevasse in Everest.
[3] Everest at sunset.
[4] Lake Gokyo, in Nepal.
[5] The peaks of Khumbu
and Ama Dablam.

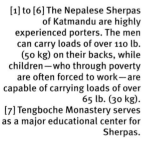

[1] to [6] The Nepalese Sherpas of Katmandu are highly experienced porters. The men can carry loads of over 110 lb. (50 kg) on their backs, while children—who through poverty are often forced to work—are capable of carrying loads of over 65 lb. (30 kg).
[7] Tengboche Monastery serves as a major educational center for Sherpas.

119

[1] The view of Everest from Pan La, in Tibet.
[2] The peak of Ama Dablam, in the Khumbu massif.
[3] and [4] A climber heading up Everest from Karta (12,139 ft./3,700 m).
[5] Everest and Makalu, on the border between Nepal and Tibet.
[6] Everest at sunset.
[7] The approach to Everest's peak.

[1], [2], and [4] The world's third highest mountain, Kangchenjunga, also known as Sewa Lungma, on the border between Sikkim and India. [3] Tea pickers on the slopes of Kangchenjunga.

[5] Trekking toward Mount Machapuchare (22,943 ft./6,993 m), in Nepal.
[6] Mountain stream in the Makalu National Park, in Nepal.
[7] Sunrise on Machapuchare.
[8] The peak of Makalu shrouded in clouds.

[Opposite page] K2, the world's second highest mountain.
[1] A climber approaching the peak of the Great Trango Tower.
[2] Climbing Gasherbrum, in Pakistan.
[3] The base camp for K2.

[1] The Karakoram Mountains, in Pakistan.
[2] and [3] K2, also called Mount Godwin-Austen.
[4] Memorial for the climbers who have died going up K2.
[5] and [6] Nanga Parbat (26,660 ft./8,126 m), also known as the "Naked Mountain," in Pakistan.

[1] The sacred plateau of Mount Kailas, in the Tibet Autonomous Region of China, attracts both Buddhist and Hindu pilgrims.
[2] The Kallas massif (22,028 ft./6,714 m), in Tibet.
[3] to [6] Mount Kallas is sacred for both Buddhists and Hindus, who call it the "Jewel of Snows." Pilgrims follow a 31-mi. (50-km) path around the mountain, in the belief that their sins will be absolved if they complete this circuit within one day.

[1] Everest at sunset.
[2] Climbing Everest.
[3] Cho Oyu (26,906 ft./8,201 m), in Tibet.

[Right] The peak of Mount Everest, free of snow.

As well as being subject to frequent and violent earthquakes, Japan is a land of volcanoes. The most famous — Mount Fuji (12,388 ft./3,776 m) — is still active, albeit at a very low level. Fuji is the most visited mountain in the world, attracting over 300,000 people every year.

Fuji is also the mountain that appears most often in the prints of great Japanese masters, as well as on postcards, tourist brochures, and countless knickknacks on sale throughout the country. This "quiet" volcano — its last eruption occurred in 1707 — is several hundred thousand years old. Its present shape dates back some 10,000 years. Fuji is a sacred mountain and for centuries women were not allowed to climb it. Samurai once set up training camps in its foothills, but these have now given way to U.S. Marine bases. The peak is covered in snow all year round, except from June to August, and in this summer period tourists and day trippers flock to climb the mountain (although most are ferried by bus to a starting point at 7,546 ft./2,300 m). In winter only experienced climbers can tackle the ascent. Mount Fuji is surrounded by five lakes and forms part of the Fuji-Hakone-Izu National Park.

Japan has other notable volcanoes, such as Hokkaido, which is still active, and Usu, which last erupted in 2000. Mount Iou is remarkable for its hot sulfurous cauldrons, where locals traditionally come to cook eggs (they are apparently more healthful this way!). The highest point of Hokkaido Island is the peak of Mount Ashi (7,513 ft./2,290 m), situated in the Daisetsu massif. Mount Ryoun is another volcano, but its magma has solidified. All these volcanoes stand within

# In the Land of the Rising Sun

the Daisetsu National Park, the biggest in Japan. Mount Fuji is not the only sacred mountain in Japan. The Three Mountains of Dewa — Yudono (4,934 ft./1,504 m), Gassan (6,509 ft./1,984 m), and Haguro (1,358 feet/414 m) — have been consecrated according to Shinto ritual and receive countless pilgrims.

[1] and [2] The slopes of Mount Fuji are covered with snow for most of the year.
[3] The crater of Mount Fuji.
[4] Mount Fuji is an active volcano.
[5] Aerial view of Mount Fuji.

[1] Mount Fuji in winter.
[2] The crater of Mount Fuji.
[3] Mount Fuji seen from Mount Hakone.

[4] Mount Fuji shrouded in mist.
[5] Mount Fuji and Lake Kawaguchi.

[1] Volcanologists in the crater of Mount Usu, on Hokkaido Island.
[2] Volcanoes in the Akan National Park, on Hokkaido Island.

[Right] Lake Motosu, at the foot of Mount Fuji.

The mountains of the Philippines attracted unwelcome attention after the unexpected eruption of Pinatubo, a volcano that had been considered extinct. It rose from its slumber in June 1991 and proceeded to spew out tons of ash and rocks for several days before petering out.

On June 15, 1991, in the paroxysm of the eruption, the peak of Pinatubo, which had risen to a height of 5,725 ft. (1,745 m), exploded in a cloud of burning rocks and smoke that shot 25 mi. (40 km) into the air, casting a gray mantle on all the surrounding area and covering Manila with ash. The volcanic activity lasted until August, when the pulverized peak of the volcano had turned into a huge lake. The smoke from the eruption went round the globe and sparked a worldwide drop in temperature of 0.2 to 0.3°C. This eruption affected over 2 million local people but fortunately caused comparatively few casualties (less than a thousand) as a massive evacuation was organized.

Not far from Manila, another volcano, Taal, poses a constant threat. It is only 1,312 ft. (400 m) high, but its frequent explosive eruptions give rise to incandescent clouds and tsunamis that make it the most deadly volcano in the country. The most active volcano in the Philippines, however, is Mayon (8,077 ft./2,462 m), which has erupted more than fifty times in less than 400 years. Its most famous eruption occurred in 1814, when the town of Cagsawa was entirely destroyed and its 1,200 inhabitants killed. The last eruption took place in August 2006, but nobody was killed as over 40,000 people were hurriedly evacuated.

The Philippines—which owe their very existence to underwater volcanic eruptions that created the 7,000 component islands—

# The Philippines

contain some twenty volcanoes that are still active, as well as many more that are extinct or dormant, such as Mount Apo (9,692 ft./2,954 m), the country's highest peak and a major tourist attraction set in the midst of a national park.

[1] Fleeing from the eruption of Mayon.
[2] and [3] Mayon has erupted more than fifty times in less than 400 years.
[4] The valleys around Mayon are extremely fertile.

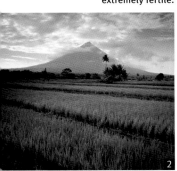

[5] and [6] Despite the dangers, many farmers live in the vicinity of Mayon.

[Folowing pages]
Terraced rice fields in Batad.

[1] Mount Apo, a volcano that emits sulfuric fumes.
[2] and [4] Terraces devoted to growing rice on the island of Luzon, a UNESCO World Heritage Site.
[3] The volcano Taal.
[5] Lake in Taal's crater.

**3** [1], [2], and [3] Trekking on the slopes of Mount Pinatubo.

[Right] Lake formed by the crater of Mount Pinatubo.

[1] The group of peaks on Pinatubo forms a circular depression known as a "caldera."
[2 to 4] The flanks of Mount Pinatubo constantly give off smoke.
[5] The caldera plays host to a lake.

Indonesia is made up of 17,000 volcanoes containing a total of 133 volcanoes, most of them still active. This archipelago boasts the highest peak in Oceania: the pyramidal Carstensz, or Puncak Jaya in the local language, which reaches 15,905 ft. (4,848 m) in the Indonesian part of New Guinea.

Sumatra, Indonesia's biggest island, has many volcanoes, particularly Kerinci (12,484 ft./3,805 m), the highest peak in the Bukit Barisan mountain range, which stretches for over 1,055 mi. (1,700 km). Other Sumatran volcanoes are still active: Dempo (10,410 feet/3,173 m), Sibayak (7,260 ft./2,213 m), Mount Talang (8,530 ft./2,600 m), and Marapi (9,485 ft./2,891 m). The latter two awoke in April 2005 after the island's northwestern region was rocked by major earthquakes—including one caused by the tsunami of December 26, 2004. The country's most dangerous volcano, however, is found on Java: Kelud (5,679 ft./1,731 m), which stands close to several built-up areas. On October 16, 2007, the Indonesian authorities ordered the evacuation of more than 30,000 people, fifteen days before Kelud started to erupt.

This volcano is complemented by several others on Java, including Arjuna (10,954 ft./3,339 m), Bromo (7,641 ft./2,329 m), and, to the south, the island's highest mountain, Semeru (12,060 ft./3,676 m). This volcano is venerated by Hindus as the dwelling place of the gods. Another sacred mountain, Agung (10,308 ft./3,142 m), is to be found on Bali, while Tambora, on the island of Sumbawa, soared to a height of 14,107 ft./4,300 m before its eruption in 1815—one of the most devastating of all time. On April 11 of that year, the summit was wrenched off by an enormous explosion, causing it to lose 4,921 ft. (1,500 m) in altitude in a few hours (it now

# The Volcanoes of Indonesia

measures 9,350 ft./2,850 m). The ash and rocks ejected from the crater formed a 100-ft. (30-m) thick layer in the surrounding area and 49,000 people were killed, either by the explosion or by the famine resulting from the destruction of crops.

[1] and [2] Rice field at the foot of Mount Agung, in Bali.

[3] Lakes Tamblingan and Buyan, at the foot of Mount Catur, in Bali.
[4] The volcano Gunung Batur.
[5] Hindu temple in Bali.

[Left] The Bukittinggi Canyon, in Sumatra.

[1] The Sianok Canyon, in Sumatra.

[1] and [2] Mount Bromo, in the National Volcano Park, Java.
[3] The smoky crater of Merapi, in Java.
[4] to [6] Incandescent lava and clouds of ash have been increasingly observed on Merapi since the tsunami of December 2004.

[1] and [2] The valleys surrounding the Kerinci volcano in Sumatra are very fertile. Their main crop is rice.

[3] The crater of Ruang, in Java.
[4] Eruption of Mount Semeru, in Java.

[1] The crater of the volcano Tagkuban, in Java.
[2] The volcanic Lake Toba, in Sumatra.

[Right] Lake Telaga Wama, on the Dieng plateau, in Java.

[Following pages] The island of Krakatoa was divided in two by a volcanic explosion in 1883.

**S**ri Lanka's most famous mountain is Adam's Peak (7,359 ft./2,243 m). It is sacred for Hindus, Buddhists, and Muslims, as it bears a cavity on its peak that is considered to be a footstep of Shiva, Buddha, or Adam by their respective congregations.

Pilgrims come every April to climb the thousands of steps leading to the top of the mountain. This tradition goes back centuries: Marco Polo described a banister made of iron chain that can still be seen to this day. Adam's Peak is not the highest mountain in Sri Lanka; this honor goes to Mount Pidurutalagala (8,281 ft./2,524 m), near Nuwara Eliya, in the center of the island. It is now out of bounds to the public, as it is being used as a military shooting range. Prior to the conflict between the Tamil Tigers of the north and the southern government, the Sri Lankan middle class used to take advantage of the cool, pleasant climate in the island's mountains to relax in a colonial setting. These mountain slopes also grow the best varieties of tea in the world.

Sri Lanka possesses other mountains clocking in at over 6,000 ft. (2,000 m): in descending order, Kirigalpattha (7,858 ft./2,395 m), Totopola (7,733 ft./2,357 m), Kudahagala (7,612 ft./2,320 m), Sripada (7,349 ft./2,240 m), Kikilimana (7,119 ft./2,170 m), Great Western (7,270 ft./2,216 m), Hakgala (7,119 ft./2,170 m), Conican Hill (7,106 ft./2,166 m), and One Tree Hill (6,890 ft./2,100 m). All these mountains are overflowing with exceptional wildlife. Their rugged landscapes are complemented by domesticated natural

# Sacred Sri Lanka

settings, such as the remarkable Lion Rock (1,214 ft./370 m) in Sigiriya, the island's royal city in the 5th century. This rock, considered the eighth Wonder of the World, is adorned with magnificent murals depicting young women in the palace of King Kassyapa (477–495). The Lion Rock is listed as a UNESCO World Heritage Site.

[1] and [2] Staircase leading pilgrims to the top of the Lion Rock.
[3] to [5] The Sigiriya frescos show women from the royal court picking lotus flowers and applying perfume to their bodies.

169

Sacred Sri Lanka

[Left] The Sigiriya rock overlooking the plain.

[1] and [2] Tea plantations on the cool, humid slopes of Nuwara Eliya.

The Caucasus Mountains are situated between the Black Sea and the Caspian Sea. This range, once known as the Atlas Mountains, is divided between South Caucasus, also known as Transcaucasia, and North Caucasus, or Ciscaucasia.

This immense barrier, 930 mi. (1,500 km) in length, is difficult to cross, as its peaks often surpass 15,000 ft. (5,000 m) in altitude, and even the lowest, the Mount of the Cross, is 7,805 ft. (2,379 m) high. The highest peak of all is Mount Elbrus, an ice-capped volcano measuring 18,511 ft. (5,642 m) that marks the frontier between Europe and Asia. Indeed, some commentators think it should be considered a European mountain and therefore deprive Mont Blanc of its title as the "roof of Europe."

On the Turkish side, the highest mountain is Mount Ararat, which comprises two peaks: one soars to 16,946 ft. (5,165 m). Legend has it that Noah's Ark came to rest here after the Flood. Mount Ararat is an inactive volcano that is covered with snow and ice all year round.

The border between Tajikistan and Kirghizistan is also straddled by a mountain: Mount Kaufmann (23,406 ft./7,134 m), which was renamed the Lenin Peak because it was long believed to be the highest mountain in the Soviet Union; it was in fact surpassed by the Ismail Samani Peak (24,590 ft./7,495 m). Kirghizistan is entirely covered by mountains, including several high peaks in the Ferghana range in the north and the Pamir range in the south. The highest of all is Pobeda Peak (24,406 ft./7,439 m). Georgia, in its turn, plays host to Mount Chkhara (16,627 ft./5,068 m) and Mount Kazbek (16,558

# The Caucasus Mountains

ft./5,047 m). Armenia is also a very mountainous country, culminating in Aragats (13,435 ft./4,095 m), an extinct volcano with four peaks. According to tradition, saints can see on its summit a divine light descending from heaven, as was the case for Saint Gregory the Illuminator when he climbed the mountain to pray.

[1] The village of Oujkouli is tucked into the valley at the base of the Elbrus massif.
[2] and [3] Mount Kazbek in Georgia, at 16,558 ft. (5,047 m) the fourth highest mountain in the Caucasus.
[4] Brick towers near Gireva, in Georgia.

175

The Middle East is the birthplace of the monotheistic religions, and several of its mountains are associated with religious symbolism. The most famous is the biblical fulcrum of Christendom, Mount Sinai, which is crowned by Saint Catherine's Mount (8,668 ft./2,642 m). The saint's body was laid here by angels after her martyrdom in Alexandria. Saint Catherine's Monastery was built at the foot of the mountain that now preserves her remains.

Mount Sinai or Jebel Musa is the mountain where Moses received the Ten Commandments for the Jewish people. Mount Carmel (1,791 ft./546 m) is mentioned in the Bible as the dwelling place of the prophet Elias. Alongside it, Keren-Hakarmel (1,555 ft./474 m) contains a Carmelite monastery that marks the site where, according to the Scriptures, Elias slaughtered Baal's disciples. Another mountain associated with the Bible, Beit Horon (1,804 ft./550 m), is famous for Joshua's victory over the five Amorite kings.

Mount Hermon (9,232 ft./2,814 m) forms part of the Anti-Lebanon range and stands at the junction of Israel, Lebanon, and Syria. The Israelis consider it their highest mountain, although internationally recognized borders grant this honor to Mount Meron (3,963 ft./1,208 m), in Galilee. Halhoul (3,366 ft./1,026 m) is one of the Mountains of Judea, situated in the middle of Israel.

Mount Tabor (1,929 ft./588 m) resembles an altar and is venerated by all three monotheist religions; according to tradition, it was the only mountain to have stayed above water during the Great Flood. The most famous mountain in Israel, however, is undoubtedly the Mount of Olives (2,713 ft./827 m), to the east of Jerusalem. It stands in

# The Middle East

the midst of the world's biggest Jewish cemetery, and it is believed that those buried on this spot once trod by the Messiah will be the first to be resurrected.

[1] View of the Sinai Desert.
[2] Saint Catherine's Monastery, at the foot of the mount of the same name.
[3] Sunrise over Mount Sinai.
[4] Soccer match at the foot of Mount Sinai, at an altitude of 7,497 ft. (2,285 m).
[5] and [6] Clouds on the summit of Mount Sinai.

[Left] A Bedouin on the slopes of Mount Sinai, leading a dromedary.

[1 to 3] Saint Catherine's Mount, also known as Jebel Katerina, attracts countless tourists and pilgrims.

[1] and [2] The arid Bawiti region is known as the Black Desert, because of its black volcanic mountains.
[3] and [right] The ancient Egyptian funeral temples of the Valley of Kings and Queens were built into the mountains in the desert.

# Mountains
# of Africa

Kilimanjaro, the highest peak
in Tanzania, overshadows the
huge expanse of Amboseli
National Park.

Tanzania is home to Africa's most famous mountain: Kilimanjaro (19,340 ft./5,895 m). Its peak, constantly topped with snow, stands in the middle of the Amboseli savannah, which is populated by elephants, gazelles, and lions. When Tanzania won its independence, the mountain was renamed Uhuru, meaning "freedom" in Swahili.

Kilimanjaro embraces the Kibo crater and the rocky pinnacles of Mawenzi, and this ensemble forms part of a magnificent national park. Kilimanjaro does not pose major challenges to experienced climbers, unless they approach the peak by the gritty slopes leading to the crater. Furthermore, hikers can climb the foothills without any difficulty to admire the extraordinary vegetation, ranging from tussock grassland to dense forests.

The Usambara Mountains (8,005 ft./2,440 m) in northeast Tanzania are subject to torrential rain that has given rise to lush tropical flora. This massif is particularly important in ecological terms, as most of the plant species found here are endemic. Both Kilimanjaro and Usambara are extinct volcanoes, as are Kitumbeine (9,400 ft./2,865 m) and Gelai (9,652 ft./2,942 m). Mount Meru, however, was still active until its last eruption in 1910; it now appears to be extinct, although it is closely monitored. Situated in northern Tanzania, it is the country's second highest peak, at 14,977 ft. (4,565 m).

Ol Doinyo (9,711 ft./2,960 m), in the Great Rift Valley is another volcano—in this case

# In the Land of Kilimanjaro

still extremely active. Its name means "Mountain of the Gods," and it is a sacred site for the Masai. The composition of its lava during eruption is unique, as it is black rather than red and then turns white when it cools, giving the impression of snow cover. Ol Doinyo last erupted on July 19, 2007.

188

[1] Kilimanjaro's crater is always topped with snow.
[2] and [3] Kilimanjaro is the highest mountain in Africa (19,340 ft./5,895 m).
[4] A church in the shadow of Kilimanjaro.
[5] The climb up Kilimanjaro is within the reach of well-prepared hikers in summer.
[6] The snow-capped peak of Kilimanjaro.

[1] Climbers camping at the foot of Kilimanjaro the night before heading to the peak.
[2] Climbers encounter glaciers on their approach to the summit.
[3] Expedition on Kilimanjaro, from Karanga to Barafu.
[4] Negotiating Kilimanjaro's lava walls.
[5] and [6] Glaciers on the peak of Kilimanjaro.

[1], [2], and [right] A Kenyan Minister of Tourism once announced that Kilimanjaro was his country's main attraction. He was forced to rectify this remark after fierce protests from Tanzania—where Kilimanjaro is in fact situated.

[1] Kilimanjaro seen from the Amboseli National Park.
[2] The savannah beneath Kilimanjaro is dotted with acacia trees.

[3] and [4] The Ol Doinyo Lengai volcano is still active. It is a sacred mountain for the Masai, who call it the "Mountain of the Gods."

[1] Lodge at the base of Ngorongoro, an extinct volcano in northern Tanzania.
[2] The Ngorongoro massif forms the world's largest caldera, some 12 ½ mi. (20 km) in diameter.
[3] The savannah at the foot of Ngorongoro is inhabited by an array of herbivores and their predators.

[1] and [2] View of Mount Mawenzi from the Barafu base camp.
[3] and [4] Mawenzi's peak is covered with glaciers.

[1] to [3] Mount Meru, in the Kilimanjaro National Park, is the second highest peak in Tanzania (14,977 ft./4,565 m).

[Opposite page] Masai in ceremonial dress attending a wedding in Arusha, Tanzania.

[Following pages] Masai at the foot of the Ol Doinyo volcano.

At 17,057 ft. (5,199 m),
Mount Kenya is the second
highest mountain in Africa.

**M**ount Kenya—called Ol Doinyo Elbor, or "White Mountain," by the Masai—culminates in two peaks, Batian (17,057 ft./5,199 m) and Nelion (17,021 ft./5,188 m), which are linked by a ledge called the "Gate of Mists." Mount Kenya is surrounded by rugged pinnacles such as Sendeyo, Tereri, and Point John, as well as glaciers such as the Lewis Glacier.

Mount Kenya, the second highest mountain in Africa, is an extinct volcano covered with glaciers. It straddles the equator, right in the middle of Kenya. The climb up this mountain involves first crossing a thick forest (richly endowed with herbs) that is home to Colobus monkeys. Higher up, at around 13,000 ft. (4,000 m), the trail passes by lakes and emerald-green moraines, lined with lobelias and numerous endemic plant species, such as the giant rosette (a succulent shrub resembling a cactus), while eagles, vultures, and Mackinder's eagle owls circle in the skies above. The next stage is the summit, complete with its glaciers (which have been steadily receding for decades).

The Diamond Corridor linking the two peaks, which was only opened in 1973, is considered the most difficult glacier in Africa to climb, but hikers can safely walk up the snowy slopes from the Lewis Glacier as far as Point Lenana (16,355 ft./4,985 m). These magnificent landscapes are protected as part of the Mount Kenya National Park, classified as a UNESCO World Heritage Site.

Kenya's frontier with Uganda is marked by a dormant volcano, Mount Elgon. Its crater, 5 mi. (8 km) in diameter, forms a base for

## Masai Country

several peaks, the highest being Wagagai, at 14,176 ft. (4,321 m). Coffee plants and banana trees grow on Elgon's fertile lower slopes, although it is largely arid above a height of 9,850 ft. (3,000 m).

[1] The high lakes of Mount Kenya are lined with giant lobelias.
[2] Mount Kenya is called the "White Mountain" by the Masai.

[3] and [4] The plains around Mount Kenya are populated by elephants.

The Democratic Republic of the Congo contains one of the most active volcanoes in the world—Nyiragongo (11,358 ft./3,462 m)—as well as the Rwenzori massif, blessed with unique vegetation and wildlife. Its highest mountain is the Margherita Peak (16,795 ft./5,119 m).

Nyiragongo forms part of the Mountains of Fire, which extend through the Congo, Rwanda, and Uganda; their highest summit is Karisimbi (14,787 ft./4,507 m), on the border between the Democratic Republic of Congo and Rwanda. Its slopes play host to the world's last mountain gorillas. Nyiragongo and its neighbor Nyamulagira (10,046 ft./3,062 m) regularly produce awesome eruptions that devastate the surrounding region. At these times a lake of lava, some 1,640 ft. (500 m) long and 656 ft. (200 m) deep, forms in the top of the volcano and then hurls out veritable bombs of lava, accompanied by deafening rumbles that shake the sides of the mountain. The locals refer to all the volcanoes in the region as virunga, which means "cooking pot." These active volcanoes are surrounded by others that are dormant or extinct, all shrouded in dense jungle.

The Rwenzori massif boasts many substantial peaks, including twenty-five with heights in excess of 13,123 ft. (4,000 m). Most are named after European monarchs and nobles, such as Alexandra, the Queen Consort of the British King Edward VII; Albert, the King of Belgium; and Luigi di Savoia, a Duke from the Abruzzi family, who was the first European to climb the Rwenzori. The path to the summit runs first through giant ragworts, then through moss and enormous

# Congo and Rwanda

ferns shrouded in thick fog. Further up, the vegetation gives way to snow and ice. The highest mountains in the Rwenzori, such as the Margherita Peak and its runner-up, the Alexandra Peak (16,762 ft./5,109 m), have been gradually losing much of their icecap for decades. The Rwenzori massif was listed as a UNESCO World Heritage Site in 1994.

[1] and [2] The Virunga National Park provides refuge for the world's last mountain gorillas. [3] Stretching for over 185 mi. (300 km), the Virunga National Park is the oldest park in Africa. [4] to [6] The Virunga National Park is constantly encroached by human beings, particularly in the form of tourist trekkers, poachers, and locals who cut down trees for firewood.

The highest peak in West Africa is Mount Cameroon (13,435 ft./4,095 m). An active volcano, it is famous for a race that attracts the world's top climbers every February.

Mount Cameroon forms part of a range of volcanoes that stretches for over 1,000 mi. (1,600 km) from the islands of Annobon, São Tomé, Principe, and Bioko to the mainland peaks of Mandara and Manengouba, a volcano 12 ½ mi. (20 km) in diameter. The last eruption of Mount Cameroon occurred on June 10, 2000. This volcano, known by the locals as the "Chariot of the Gods," contains more than 100 cones that regularly emit lava. Its slopes are therefore enriched by lava, and this phenomenon, combined with heavy rainfall, makes them extremely fertile. Consequently, the region has become renowned for the superb quality of its cacao trees. On the upper slopes of Mount Cameroon (from 9,200 ft./2,800 m), only moss and lichen can survive.

Mount Oku (9,875 ft./3,010 m) and its neighbor Kilum-ljim (8,202 ft./2,500 m) are situated in northwest Cameroon. The sides of Mount Oku are covered with the largest expanse of mountain forest in Africa, replete with many species not found elsewhere, such as the Mount Oku rat (*Lamottemys okuensis*), a small rodent only discovered in 1986 and now under threat of extinction. Fifteen species of birds also live in this forest, alongside exceptional plant life, including numerous types of bamboo and *Rubiaceae*, a family of flowering plants. This region is densely populated, and the resulting pressure on natural resources has led to severe deforestation. To halt this decline, the forest has been declared a nature reserve and research programs into its flora and fauna are now under way, in collaboration with the some of the world's major museums, particularly London's Natural History Museum.

# Cameroon

[1] to [3] The Mandara Mountains in northern Cameroon are in the center of the Kingdom of Wandala, founded in 1500 by the Mandarawa people.
[4] Mount Cameroon in eruption, seen from the peak of Little Cameroon (4,921 ft./1,500 m).
[5] Mount Cameroon is called the "Chariot of the Gods" by the local people.
[6] An annual race on Mount Cameroon attracts hundreds of athletes from all over the world, intent on outclimbing their rivals over a course that runs up and down the mountain.

The highest peak in South Africa is Thabana Ntlenyana, which literally means "Pretty Little Black Mountain" (even though it soars to a height of 11,424 ft./3,482 m). It forms part of the Drakensberg Mountains, which stretch for over 620 mi. (1,000 km) from Natal to the Transvaal.

Drakensberg is an Afrikaans name meaning "Dragon Mountain"; the Zulu term is "Quathlamba," or the "Rampart of Spears." Other massifs crown Africa's southernmost tip, such as that of Table Mountain in Cape Province, which rises to 3,563 ft. (1,086 m). It is flanked by two hills, Lion's Head and Signal Hill. This particular massif is protected within a national park and is very popular with hikers–although less energetic visitors can reach the peak in a cable car. Table Mountain is the only mountain to have given its name to a constellation, which was first sighted from its peak by the astronomer Nicolas Louis de la Caille.

The Witwatersrand, meaning the "Crest of the White Waters" in Afrikaans, is a low massif, as its highest peak registers only 5,837 ft. (1,779 m). These mountains are famous for their gold mines; in the 1920s they provided 40 percent of the world's gold. Furthermore, this region, popularly known as the Rand, gave its name to South Africa's official currency, the rand.

The Witwatersrand Mountains also constitute a natural barrier between a desert area

# South Africa

and another, much lusher one, as well as separating the Atlantic Ocean from the Indian Ocean. The South African mountains venerated by the Zulus are rigorously protected as they stand within natural parks. The country boasts seven UNESCO World Heritage Sites, four of them natural sites and three of them cultural monuments.

[1] The Drakensberg Mountains are situated in Zulu territory.
[2] Natal National Park.
[3] Village at the foot of the Drakensberg Mountains.
[4] The Drakensberg Mountains: their highest peak is Thabana Ntlenyana (11,424 ft./3,482 m).
[5] Zulus in Natal.

[1] and [2] Mountain lakes in the Natal National Park. [3] Hikers' lodge on the way to the Drakensberg Mountains.

[4] and [5] Zulu territory in Natal, overlooked by the Drakensberg Mountains.
[6] Hiker in the Natal National Park.

[Following pages] The Drakensberg Mountains.

Mount Ras Dashan, Africa's
fourth highest peak,
is situated in the Simien
National Park.

The Ethiopian trappa are volcanic plateaux resulting from an accumulation of lava that occurred over a period of 30 million years. These plateaux give rise to mountains, the highest of which is Ras Dashan (14,872 ft./4,533 m).

Ras Dashan is the fourth highest mountain in Africa. Its peak consists of grayish rocks devoid of vegetation. Further down, on the plain, vegetation starts to appear and the cool, humid climate is ideally suited to agriculture, with coffee as the main crop. Ras Dashan is also the source of several rivers, including the Blue Nile. Further north, Amba Alagi (12,956 ft./3,949 m) is famous for being the site of various battles: the Ethiopian victory against the Italians in 1895; another Italian defeat in 1941, this time at the hands of British troops during World War II; and a rebellion in 1943.

Woyane Erta Ale (2,011 ft./613 m), the "Smoking Mountain," is a small shield volcano in the north of the Great Rift Valley that is still active; its last eruption occurred in 1967. Although it is not very high, it is over 18 ½ mi. (30 km) in diameter. It forms part of a chain stretching for over 55 mi. (90 km) that also includes Gafa Ale, Alu-Dala Filla, Borale Ale, Hayli Gub, and Ale Bagu.

The Afars believe that the "Smoking Mountain" harbors evil spirits and never go near it. It is in fact extremely inaccessible and was first surveyed as recently as the 1960s, mainly by Haroun Tazieff, the famous French

# Ethiopia and Chad

volcanologist who discovered its lakes of lava. Since his first sighting, the surface levels of these lakes have risen inexorably and lava often overflows from the crater. In the same area, Fentale (6,585 ft./2,007 m) is considered an active volcano, but its two known eruptions date back to the seventeenth and nineteenth centuries.

**3**

[1] Gelada monkeys are unique to the plateaus of Eritrea and Ethiopia.
[2] Ethiopian wolves are not found outside the country.
[3] View of the Asmara Mountains, in Ethiopia.

[4] Isolated Ethiopian village on the top of an escarpment.
[5] Transporting food and materials to remote mountain villages in Ethiopia.

[1] Tourists on the cooled lava of an Ethiopian volcano.
[2] An itinerant trader in the Simien Mountains, in Ethiopia.
[3] Crater of a volcano in the Simien massif.
[4] Haroun Tazieff, the famous French volcanologist, on one of the craters of Erta Ale, in Ethiopia.

[Following pages] Camel driver at the foot of the Trou au Natron volcano, in Chad.

[1] Crater of the Trou au Natron volcano.
[2] The Soborom volcano (10,171 ft./3,100 m), in Chad.
[3] The Zoumri massif, in Chad.
[4] and [5] The Ehi Atroun Mountain, in Chad.
[6] The Trou au Natron volcano.

Peak in the Atakor massif,
the highest massif in the
Hoggar Mountains.

The Sahara, the world's biggest desert, stretches from the Atlantic to the Red Sea, and from the Mediterranean to the Sahel. It is much more than just mile after mile of sand dunes, however: it also contains a series of massifs that make up the Atlas Mountains.

This mountain range is divided into three main massifs: the Moroccan Atlas, the Saharan Atlas, and the Tell Atlas. The highest peaks are found in the Moroccan Atlas, which is further divided into the Middle Atlas, the High Atlas, and the Anti-Atlas. The highest of all is Jebel Toubkal (13,671 ft./ 4,167 m), in the High Atlas, in Morocco. This mountain attracts many hikers every year because it is easy to climb, especially as porters are on hand to lend their services to tourists.

The highest peak in the Middle Atlas is Jebel Bou Naceur (11,010 ft./3,356 m), followed by Mouâsker (10,587 ft./3,227 m); that in the Anti-Atlas is Jebel Sirwa (10,843 ft./3,305 m). The Saharan Atlas culminates at 7,336 ft. (2,236 m) with the Djebel Aissa, in Algeria, a country that also contains the Garet El Djenoum, or the "Mountain of the Spirits" (7,644 ft./2,330 m). This peak to the north of the Hoggar Mountains is flanked by the monolithic Takouba, also known as the Tuareg Sword, and by In Acoulmou (7,664 feet/2,336 m).

The highest mountain in Algeria is Tahat (9,573 ft./2,918 m). Its rock faces bear wall paintings dating back to 10,000–8,000 BC. These depict animals in a lush setting—proof of the climatic changes that have affected the region. The Tell Atlas extends for over 4,350

# The Atlas Mountains

ft. (7,000 km) along the coast and their highest peak is Lalla Khadija (7,572 ft./2,308 m). In Kabilia, the longest chain of mountains is the Djurdjura, over 60 mi. (100 km) long. To the northwest stands Ouarsenis (6,512 ft./ 1,985 m), which plays host to the most beautiful cedar (Cedrus atlantica) forest in the Atlas Mountains.

[1] and [4] Basalt peaks in the Hoggar
Mountains, near Assekrem, in Algeria.
[2] Peak in the Atakor massif.

[Following pages] Toubkal massif,
in Morocco.

237

[1] An oasis in Morocco.
[2] A Berber at the foot of the snow-capped peaks of the Toubkal massif.
[3] View of Agdz, in Morocco.

[4] The Moroccan town of Timerhir in a valley in the High Atlas.
[5] Mountains in the High Atlas, in Morocco.

242

[1] Tourist road in the High Atlas.
[2] Snow-capped peaks in the High Atlas.
[3] Berber village backing onto a mountain in the High Atlas.
[4] Peaks in the High Atlas in the summer.
[5] Road on a valley in the High Atlas.
[6] Walker on a peak in the High Atlas.

[1] to [3] Hikers in the High Atlas.

[Opposite page] Climbing a rock in the High Atlas with bare hands.

Mountains
of the Americas

**A**laska is sliced by three mountain ranges. The coastal range, 1,180-mi. (1,900-km) long, starts with the Panhandle and finishes near Anchorage. The Brooks Range isolates the country from the Great North, while the Alaska Range is dominated by Mount McKinley.

Mount McKinley, called Denali (or "the Highest") by the indigenous people, is indeed the highest peak in North America. It stands inside a huge national park and is surrounded by numerous glaciers and mountain lakes. It is very difficult to climb, largely on account of the extreme climatic conditions on its peak, as the temperature can drop to -68 °F (-56 °C). Mount McKinley is one of the "Seven Sisters," the title bestowed on the highest peaks from each continent. It stands close to other mighty peaks such as Mount Foraker (17,401 ft./5,304 m), Mount Hunter (14,573 ft./4,442 m), and Mount Hayes (13,832 ft./4,216 m).

Another large natural park contains the Aleutian Mountains, complete with active volcanoes. This area, known as the "Land of Fires," has experienced many earthquakes, including one in June 1912 that undermined the Falling Mountain (hence its name). This cataclysm was triggered by the eruption of the volcano Katmai (7,480 ft./2,280 m) on June 6; this caused the ground to open and give rise to a new volcano, later christened

## Alaska or the Great North

Novarupta. The volcanic activity and earth tremors lasted for more than a week, and the resulting tons of incandescent lava took years to cool. To the north, the Brooks Range culminates at 9,019 ft. (2,749 m) with Mount Chamberlin, situated in the Great North national reserve, spread over 13,000 sq. mi. (33,600 km²).

[1] The Denali National Park, distinguished by hundreds of glaciers, spans over 6 million acres (2,400,000 hectares).
[2] Climber on top of Mount McKinley.
[3] The Denali National Park is served by a network of roads that are often covered with snow.

**[4]** Mount McKinley is subjected to icy winds and thick fog.
**[5]** Melting ice from Mount McKinley feeds the River Chulitna.
**[6]** A bus takes tourists along a winding road to the foot of Mount McKinley.

[1] and [2] The tundra below Mount McKinley is covered with lichen and heather.
[3] Wonder Lake, at the foot of Mount McKinley.

[4] Threatening clouds loom over the Denali National Park.
[5] Denali Park can provide surprises for hikers—in this case, an encounter with a grizzly bear.
[6] A mountain road leading to the Polychrome Pass.

253

[1] The Kahiltna glacier, with Mount McKinley and Mount Foraker.
[2] Mount Foraker, in the Denali National Park.

[3] The Ruth Glacier, in the Denali National Park.
[4] Eruption of the volcano Veniaminof.
[5] The Cook Inlet estuary covers over 3,900 sq. mi. (10,000 km²). It is bounded by four active volcanoes.

[1] The slopes of Mount Fairweather (15,325 ft./4,671 m).
[2] Glacier on Mount Fairweather.
[3] Glacier Riggs in the Glacier Bay National Park.

[Right] On July 9, 1958, an avalanche on Mount Fairweather triggered a tsunami.

[1] Sleighs drawn by dogs provide the most efficient means of transport through the glaciers of Mount McKinley.
[2] The Dall mountain sheep, a species endemic to Alaska.
[3] Caribou are not afraid of the icy water in the lakes around Mount McKinley.

[4] The tundra provides the caribou with berries to eat in the fall.
[5] Epilobiums grow extensively in the cool, damp areas around the mountain lakes.
[6] Aspens produce attractive red blossoms in the fall.

Yellowstone Park is famous
for its hot springs: here, the
Mammoth Hot Springs.

The Rocky Mountains begin in Canada and then extend for over 3,000 mi. (4,800 km) across the American states of Washington, Montana, Wyoming, Idaho, Colorado, and New Mexico. The highest of the peaks on the U.S. side is Mount Elbert (14,439 ft./4401 m), in Colorado.

The Rocky Mountains were formed 70 million years ago after the collision of the Pacific and North American tectonic plates. Native Americans such as the Apache, Bannock, Cheyenne, and Sioux peoples all considered these mountains sacred.

# The Rocky Mountains

The highest Canadian Rockies are Mount Logan (19,583 ft./5,969 m), the highest peak in the entire country, and Mount Robson (12,972 ft./3,954 m). In the Cascades range, Mount Saint Helens was responsible for a devastating eruption on May 18, 1980, when an explosion 500 times more powerful than that of the atom bomb dropped on Hiroshima ejected a gigantic column of smoke, ash, and burning rock. The volcano's peak exploded, reducing its height from 9,524 ft. (2,903 m) to 8,232 ft. (2,509 m).

The less combustible Grand Teton (13,770 ft./4,197 m), in Wyoming, is the centerpiece for one of America's most beautiful national parks, the Grand Teton National Park. Heading south, Colorado boasts fifty-four mountains of over 14,000 ft. (4,267 m). Apart from Mount Elbert, these include Mount Harvard (14,419 ft./4,395 m), Mount Massive (14,419 ft./4,395 m), and Blanca Peak (14,390 ft./4,386 m). The Rockies end in New Mexico with the Sandia Mountains, where the highest peak is the Sandia Crest (10,679 ft./3,255 m). The word Sandia means "watermelon" in Spanish, and it is apparently derived from the red color given off by the rocks at sundown.

[1] to [3] The State of Wyoming possesses one of the most beautiful natural parks in the United States: the Grand Teton National Park.

[4] The Jackson Hole Historic Museum chronicles life in this part of the Rockies.
[5] Ranch in Wyoming, in the shadow of the Rocky Mountains.
[6] Horses still provide the best means of discovering the vast expanses of the Grand Teton National Park.

[Left] Longs Peak reflected in Bear Lake, Colorado.

[1 to 3] Longs Peak (14,258 ft./4,346 m) forms part of the 545 "fourteeners" in the Rocky Mountains. Its slopes are covered with dense evergreen forest.

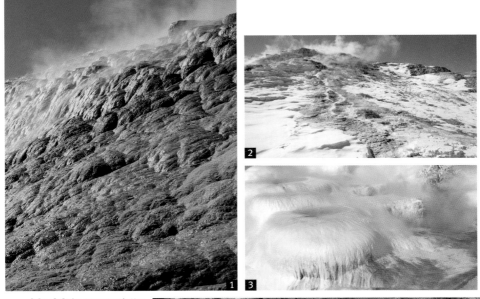

[1] to [4] The Mammoth Hot Springs in Yellowstone Park attract numerous tourists—as well as elks, which come here to bathe.

[5] Wheeler Peak (13,159 ft./4,011 m) is the highest mountain in New Mexico. It is situated at southern end of the Rockies.

[6] The red rocks of this mountain on the border between New Mexico and Colorado have earned it the name of Sangre de Cristo (Blood of Christ).

[1] and [2] Granite boulders on Pikes Peak (14,111 ft./4,301 m) in Colorado.
[3] Hikers on the peak of Mount Evans (14,262 ft./4,347 m) in Colorado.

[4] and [5] The Garden of the Gods, at the foot of Pikes Peak, in Colorado, is extremely popular with visitors.

[Left] Mount Elbert, in Colorado, is the highest peak in the Rocky Mountains (14,439 ft./4,401 m).
[1] Signpost pointing the way to the top of Mount Logan, the highest peak in Canada.
[2] and [3] Alpine plants grow at heights of up to 11,483 ft. (3,500 m) on Mount Logan.
[4] This winding road climbs up to Logan Pass (6,562 ft./2,000 m).
[Following pages] Climbers face a daunting challenge with Mount Robson in Canada, especially on its icy wall known as the Emperor Face.

[Left] and [1] Lake Almanor and Mount Lassen, in the Cascades Mountains.
[2] Mount Lassen is a dormant volcano that reaches a height of 10,456 ft. (3,187 m).

[Following pages]
Mount Rainier, in the Washington National Park.

[1] to [3] Mount Rainier is an active volcano in the Cascades Mountain, in Washington State.

[4] to [6] Mount Rainier is a permanent danger for Seattle, which has a population of 1.5 million inhabitants.

[1] to [3] The slopes and valleys of Mount Rainier are dotted with a wide variety of flowers.

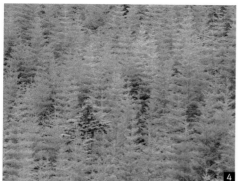

[4] and [5] Mount Rainier is surrounded by thick forests of Douglas fir.
[6] The slopes of Mount Rainier are still covered with snow in spring, while the surrounding valleys are covered with flowers.

[Following pages]
Night falls on Seattle, with the threat of Mount Rainier in the background.

[1] and [2] The lake formed by the eruption of Mount Saint Helens.

[3] and [4] Eruption of Mount Saint Helens in the summer of 1980.
[5] Mount Saint Helens, capped with snow and asleep once again.

The rushing waters of the
Ausabie River are highly prized
by kayak enthusiasts.

T he Appalachian Mountains are situated in North America. They stretch for 2,175 mi. (3,500 km) from Newfoundland in Canada to North Carolina and then South Alabama. Their highest peak is Mount Mitchell (6,683 ft./2,037 m).

Mount Mitchell is named after Elisha Mitchell, who was the first to measure it and subsequently fell to his death from its heights in 1857. He was buried on the mountain bearing his name, and his tomb on the peak is constantly adorned with flowers. The climb up Mount Mitchell is facilitated by well-kept footpaths with clear signposts. The conditions are tough in winter, however, as the temperature can drop to -40 °F (-40 °C), with fierce winds that can reach speeds of up to 178 mph (286 kph).

The origins of the Appalachians can be traced back to the Primary Era. The region is rich in sediments with thick seams of coal, which were long its main source of wealth. To the east the mountains are distinguished by their hard rock—such as quartzite, particularly in the Blue Ridge Mountains (6,500 ft./2,000 m)—but further south the rock becomes softer and crystalline. This geological configuration of alternating hard and soft rock in a pleated mountain structure is known as Appalachian relief.

The Appalachian region, which once thrived on metallurgy and was one of the richest in the Unites States, has become the

# The Appalachians

"black country," ailing on account of its industrial decline. The Appalachian Trail, an extraordinary footpath over 2,175 mi. (3,500 km) long, passes through eleven states, making it possible to walk from Mount Springer (3,271 ft./997 m) in Georgia to Mount Katahdin (5,269 ft./1,606 m) in Maine.

**3**

[1] Mount Mitchell is the highest peak in the Appalachians.
[2] Mount Mitchell seen from the Great Craggy.
[3] The White Mountains are very popular with visitors from nearby Boston and New York.

[Right] Lake Echo, in British Columbia, is famous for its abundant supply of fish.

**3** [Opposite page] A lake lined with lupins, in the White Mountains.

[1] The snow-capped peak of Pinkham Notch, in the White Mountains.
[2] A climber tackles a vertical wall of ice.
[3] Mount Kinsman, in the White Mountains.

[1] Mount Washington, in the White Mountains.
[2] A granite rock against the backdrop of Mount Washington and Mount Adams.
[3] Mount Washington.

[4] and [5] The Gros Mome National Park runs alongside the Gulf of Saint Lawrence, in Canada.
[6] Mount Katahdin, in Maine.

[1] The Berkshire Hills seen from Mount Greylock, in Massachusetts.
[2] and [right] The peak of Mount Mansfield, in the Green Mountains, Vermont.

[1] Hikers on the top of the Stony Man, in the Shenandoah National Park.
[2] Waterfall in the Blue Ridge Mountains, North Carolina.
[3] The peak of Mount Mitchell, shrouded in mist.

[4] The Blue Ridge Mountains, in North Carolina.
[5] Great Smoky Mountains, in Tennessee.
[6] Table Rock Mountains, in North Carolina.

The Half Dome is one of the
wonders of the Yosemite
National Park in California.

The Sierra Nevada is a mountain range in eastern California. As well as possessing some spectacular peaks, it harbors the famous Death Valley and, in the White Mountains, the famous bristlecone pines, the world's oldest trees, dating back more than 5,000 years.

Mount Whitney (14,505 ft./4,421 m) is the highest mountain in the Sierra Nevada. It stands not far from the scorching desert of Death Valley, but its peak is permanently covered with snow. ("Sierra Nevada" means "Snowy Mountain Range.") This range is also famous for the Yosemite Park, complete with two granite mountains that attract the world's best climbers: El Capitán and the Half Dome, which were discovered by John Muir. He was the first to climb Cathedral Peak (in 1869) and fought to protect these mountains— hence the creation of the Yosemite Park in 1890. The vertical wall of the Half Dome remained unconquered until 1957. El Capitán has also attracted thrill seekers, particularly on its Nose, a vertical pillar 3,937 ft. (1,200 m) high that divides the mountain into two.

Other high peaks in the Sierra Nevada include Mount Williamson (14,403 ft./4,390 m), the North Palisade (14,242 ft./4,341 m), Mount Sill (14,154 ft./4,314 m), and Mount Muir (14,012 ft./4,271 m). In the southwest part of the park, the Sierra Nevada succors

# The Sierra Nevada

the oldest trees in the world, on the top of the White Mountains, at heights of above 13,000 ft. (4,000 m). They are the only trees able to withstand both the dry, torrid heat of summer and the intense cold of winter. To the south, the Sequoia National Park protects the last surviving giant sequoias, over 3,000 years old and over 260 ft. (80 m) high.

**3** [1] and [3] El Capitán is a granite monolith, 7,569 ft. (2,307 m) high. It poses a daunting challenge to climbers.
[2] The valleys in the Yosemite Park play host to dense forest.

[4] to [6] Carl Boenish , the inventor of base jumping—a sport that involves leaping from a fixed point into a void with a parachute—made his first jump from the peak of El Capitán, in the Yosemite Park. This discipline is now considered the ultimate in extreme sport.

[1] The Half Dome is topped with snow in winter.
[2] and [3] The River Merced runs underneath the Half Dome, inviting visitors to take a dip.

[4] View of the south face of the Half Dome.
[5] View of the Tenaya Canyon in the Yosemite National Park.
[6] The Yosemite National Park was declared a UNESCO World Heritage Site in 1984.

[Opposite page] Sunset on the Half Dome.

[1] A delta plane flying above the Yosemite Park.
[2] Waterfall in the Yosemite Park.

[Left] The Young Lakes form a group of three lakes in the Yosemite Park.

[1] Mount Conness, in the Yosemite Park.
[2] The Yosemite Park contains numerous waterfalls, including some of the highest in the world. The Bridalveil Falls are particularly impressive.
[3] One of the Young Lakes, at the foot of Mount Conness.

[1] to [3] The Yosemite Park boasts exceptional plant life, including numerous species of lily.
[4] Transporting goods on horseback in the Virginia Lakes valley.

[5] and [6] The Yosemite Park has an abundance of giant sequoias; some are thousands of years old and over 260 ft. (80 m) high.
[7] The *Castilleja densiflora* is a semi-parasitical plant endemic to California.

[1] and [2] The climb up Mount Whitney is one of the most difficult in the Sierra Nevada. [3] Mount Whitney (14,505 ft./4,421 m) is the highest peak in the Sierra Nevada.

[4] and [5] A reddish desert stretches out at the foot of the snow-capped Mount Whitney.

[Following pages]
The mountains around Mount Whitney overlook the Owens Valley.

The Sierra Madre is the prolongation of the Sierra Nevada. This mountain range, largely situated in Mexico, is subject to violent seismic activity, as well as possessing the highest volcanic peaks in the Americas.

Although Ixtaccihuatl, which culminates at 17,342 ft. (5,286 m), is an extinct volcano, this is not true of Popocatepetl (17,887 ft./5,452 m), the name of which means "Smoking Mountain." Popo, as it is commonly known, erupted some thirty times but after the nineteenth century it appeared to be dormant—until it renewed its activity in 1994, forcing the Mexican authorities to evacuate the population close to the mountain. (Popo is only a few miles from Mexico City.) According to the experts, a greater eruption is expected in the coming years. The first ascent of Popo took place in 1523, when Cortez was out of gunpowder and sent his soldiers to look for sulfur in the volcano's crater.

The Colima volcano (12,533 ft./3,820 m), situated 435 mi. (700 km) from Mexico City, is highly active. In June 2005 it spewed out ashes for a distance of 27,887 ft. (8,500 m), but the eruption caused no casualties. Ixtaccihuatl has four peaks, which according to Aztec legend represent the head, chest, knees, and feet of a princess who fell in love with one of her father's soldiers. The king promised his daughter that if the soldier came back alive from the wars, then she could marry him. The king was opposed to the marriage, however, and made the princess believe that her beloved had died

# The Sierra Madre

on the battlefield, causing her to die of a broken heart. When the soldier returned from the war, he also died of grief. The gods covered the two dead lovers with snow and turned them into mountains: the princess became Ixtaccihuatl and the soldier Popocatepetl, venting his rage and torment ever since.

[1] The Mexican town of Batopilas is situated at the bottom of a canyon of the same name.
[2] A church was built near Saveto, in the Sierra Madre, to bring the gospel to the indigenous people.
[3] The Sierra Tarahumara is a mountainous area that forms part of the western Sierra Madre.

[4] The Sierra Madre is a desert region dotted with cacti.
[5] A hiker admires the Copper Canyon.
[6] The mountain slopes in the Sierra Madre often comprise vertical walls.

[Following pages]
The western Sierra Madre.

[1] and [2] The volcano Colima, situated 435 mi. (700 km) from Mexico City, has been highly active since 1999.
[3] Volcanologists collect gas samples from Colima's crater.

[4 to 6] The snow-capped peak of the volcano Popocatepetl gives off smoke, posing a great threat to Mexico City, which is only a few dozen miles away.

The *altiplano*, or high
mountain plateau,
is inhabited by llamas.

# The Andes

The Andes is the world's longest mountain range, stretching from the Caribbean to Tierra del Fuego. It is a succession of very distinct massifs — from soaring peaks like Aconcagua to active volcanoes such as Cotopaxi.

Aconcagua, in Argentina, is the roof of the Americas, with a height of 22,841 ft. (6,962 m). It is the highest point in the southern hemisphere. Its name means "Stone Mountain" in the language of the Huarpa Indians. Its southern face, 8,202 ft. (2,500 m) high and 3 mi. (5 km) wide, is constantly swept by huge avalanches. Further south, close to Cape Horn, the Andes come to an end with the Cerro Torre (10,262 ft./3,128 m), Mount Fitz Roy (11,289 ft./3,441 m), and the massif of the Torres del Paine (8,202 ft./2,500 m). In the midst of the ice of Patagonia, these granite mountains are surrounded by peaks and towers such as the Cerro Adela and the Torre Egger.

The Atlantic slopes are characterized by the Grande, Piedras Blancas, and Marconi glaciers. All this part of the Andes is the habitat of the condor, a rare, majestic bird. At the other end, to the north, Ecuador possesses a series of volcanoes that were described by the naturalist Humboldt as the "Boulevard of Volcanoes." The highest is Chimborazo (20,702 ft./6,310 m), followed by Cotopaxi (19,347 ft./5,897 m); the latter is still active, and is known as the "Fire Mountain." Its last eruption, in 1905, completely destroyed the town of Latacunga.

Going further down toward Peru, the Cordillera Blanca contains Alpamayo (19,511 ft./5,947 m) and Huascarán (22,205 ft./6,768 m), which are surrounded by over 600 glaciers, all located within the bounds of the 840,000-acre (340,000-ha) Huascarán National Park. Bolivia also boasts some imposing peaks, such as Illimani (21,201 ft./6,462 m), which is covered with walls of ice and enormous crevices that make it very difficult to climb.

[1] Peaks of the Fitz Roy Mountains in Argentina, culminating at a height of 11,289 ft. (3,441) m.
[2] The Fitz Roy Mountains are situated in Los Glaciares National Park.
[3] and [4] The Cerro Torre brings the Andes to an end in Patagonia.
[5] Sunset with moon on the Patagonian Andes.

[6] A waterfall down the slopes of Mount Fitz Roy feeds the Arroyo del Salto River.
[7] View of Mount Fitz Roy and the Cerro Torre in Los Glaciares National Park.
[8] Aconcagua, in Argentina, is the highest peak in the Americas.

[1] The Perito Moreno glacier in Argentina extends for over 3 mi. (5 km) and plunges 200 ft. (60 m) below the water level.
[2] Climbing the icy slopes of Aconcagua.
[3] The Cayambe volcano in Ecuador is covered with snow all year round.

[4] High-mountain rapids rushing down the slopes of Fitz Roy.
[5] The green waters of a high lake in Los Glaciares National Park.
[6] Andean mountains in Peru.

[1] The Cayambe volcano in Ecuador dominates the Zuleta Valley.
[2] El Chaltén, in Patagonia.
[3] Climbing Aconcagua from the Pass of Los Horcones.
[4] Nevado Ancohuma and Illampu, in Bolivia.

[5] Cemetery on the high plane (*altiplano*) in Bolivia.
[6] Five of the six members of the French expedition that conquered Aconcagua in 1953 had several fingers and toes amputated.
[7] Chimborazo is a volcano in Ecuador that rises to a height of 20,112 ft. (6,130 m).
[8] Road leading to the top of Mount Fitz Roy.

[1] Mount Illimani looms over the city of La Paz.
[2] and [3] Cayambe is clearly visible from Quito, the capital of Ecuador.

[Opposite page] Achacachi, at the foot of Mount Illimani in Bolivia, is one of the highest towns in the world.

[All the photos] Machu Picchu, in Peru, stands on a promontory over 7,874 ft. (2,400 m) high. It contains the ruins of an Inca sanctuary and was classified as a UNESCO World Heritage Site in 1983.

# Mountains of
# Oceania and
# Antarctica

Ayers Rock stands, red and
mysterious, within the Uluru
National Park in Australia.

**A**ustralia has only one chain of mountains: the Great Dividing Range, stretching from northeast Queensland to the Grampian Mountains in east Victoria. The country's most famous mountain, however, is undoubtedly Ayers Rock.

Mount Kosciuszko (7,310 ft./2,228 m) is the highest peak in the Great Dividing Range (although the active volcano Mawson Peak on Heard Island is, at 9,006 ft. (2,745 m), the highest point on Australian territory). The term "mountain range" is not strictly appropriate in this case, however, as these mountains are not of one piece. Their main components are the Blue Mountains, the Snowy Mountains, and the Victorian Alps. The great age of these mountains and the effects of erosion have made Australian peaks easy to climb, with Mount Kosciuszko one of the easiest of all.

The MacDonnell Mountains, over 800 million years old, can even be climbed by children, although their peaks are quite substantial (for example, Mount Zeil, at 5,023 ft. (1,531 m) , and Mount Sonder, at 4,527 ft. (1,380 m). Saint Mary Peak (3,839 ft./1,170 m) in the Flinders Range, in South Australia, is one of the Aboriginals' sacred rocks, although the most venerated of all is Ayers Rock. This huge mound, 2,848 ft. (868 m) high, seems to have been dropped into the middle of the desert. It stands alone as a monolith or, in geological terms, an inselberg ("island-mountain").

There are dozens of inselbergs in the world, such as Suilven in Scotland, Monadnock in New Hampshire, and, most famously, the Sugar Loaf Mountain overlooking the bay of Rio de Janeiro in Brazil. As in the case of icebergs, the visible portion of an insel-

# Australia's Great Dividing Range

berg represents less than a third of its mass, as the rest is buried in the ground. Ayers Rock, made of sandstone encrusted with iron particles, changes color over the course of a day, and gives off a particularly spectacular ocher color at dawn and at dusk.

Ayers Rock is one of the most frequently visited mountains in the world, as well as being an Australian national monument and a sacred Aboriginal site.

338

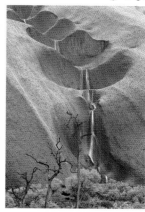

[Opposite page] The North Falls are located high in the mountains and their waters are extremely icy.

[1] Mount Hotham (6,106 ft,/1,861 m) is the highest point in the Victorian Alps.
[2] The Three Sisters stand close to Sydney, in the Blue Mountains.

Mount Cook, the highest point
in New Zealand, towers above
Lake Pukaki.

N ew Zealand is endowed with several mountain ranges, the longest being the so-called Southern Alps. These also provide the highest peaks, with eighteen above 9,800 ft. (3,000 m). Mount Cook is the highest of all, at 12,316 ft. (3,754 m).

Mount Cook, also known as Aoraki, is situated within a region called Te Wahipounamu, which became a national park in 1953 and is now a UNESCO World Heritage Site. This park also contains Mount Aspiring, or Tititea to the Maoris (9,951 ft./3,033 m), Mount Pollux (8,340 ft./2,542 m), and Mount Brewster (8,264 ft./2,519 m). The range of the Remarkables, with the crowning peak of the Double Cone (7,677 ft./2,340 m), rises up close to Queenstown. Northern New Zealand is blessed with Mount Hikurangi (5,755 ft./1,754 m), the Maoris' sacred mountain which shelters the canoe of the legendary hero Maui.

Mount Ruapehu, an active volcano (9,176 ft./2,797 m) in the center of the North Island, possesses several peaks and is surrounded by the Tongariro National Park. It is 200,000 years old and erupts regularly (roughly every two years). Mount Taranaki, or Mount Egmont (8,261 ft./2,518 m), is a dormant volcano that forms part of a group of volcanoes called the Kaitoke Range. Mount Banks is an extremely old, extinct volcano in the Canterbury region that has been eroded to form a peninsula, where the highest peak is Mount Herbert (3,016 ft./919 m). New Zealand also boasts another superlative the mountain with the longest name in the world: Tetaumatawhakatangihangakoauaotamateaure-

# The Alps of New Zealand

haeaturipukapihimaungahoronukupokaiwhenuaakitanarahu. This is the Maori name for a hill (1,000 ft./305 m) on the North Island; it can be translated as "the peak where Tamatea, the big-kneed man, the mountain climber, the tireless walker, played the flute to a loved one." For the sake of simplicity, the locals refer to it as Taumata!

[All photos] Mount Cook belongs to the Te Wahipounamu National Park, which was classified as a UNESCO World Heritage Site in 1990. It contains many mountains of over 6,500 ft. (2,000 m) in height, as well as numerous glaciers and lakes.

[1] Sand and dust on the sides of the Ruapehu volcano.
[2] The Ngauruhoe volcano, the highest peak in the Tongariro massif.
[3] Volcanoes in the Tongariro massif.

4
5

6 [4] and [5] Mount Ngaurohoe, an active volcano on the Tongariro massif.
[6] The Tongariro massif covered by clouds.

[Opposite page], [1], and [2]
The Maoris' Mount Taranaki is
called Mount Egmont by
English speakers. It is a
dormant volcano in the Kaitoke
Range.

Bagana volcano on the island
of Bougainville, in Papua
New Guinea.

**N**ew Guinea is the second largest island in the world, after Greenland. The third largest, Borneo, is shared politically by Indonesia, Malaysia, and the Sultanate of Brunei. Both these islands boast several massifs with an abundance of exceptional plant and animal life.

Mount Kinabalu (13,435 ft./4,095 m), situated in the state of Sabah in northeast Borneo, is particularly famous for its extraordinary flora, much of it endemic. The most remarkable species to be found on its slopes are the Nepentheae, carnivorous plants with deadly cavities several feet high. This mountain is also renowned for its orchids, including the celebrated Paphiopedilum rothschildianum, a component of many hybrids. The highest peak in New Guinea forms part of the Sudirman Mountains, in Papua: Puncak Jaya (16,532 ft./5,039 m), also known as the Carstensz Pyramid. This mountain is not only the highest in Oceania, but also the second highest peak in Southeast Asia, after Hkakabo Razi (19,295 ft./5,881 m), in Burma.

Papua possesses volcanoes that are still very active, such as Karkar (6,033 ft./1,839 m), which last erupted in August 1979, and Tavurvur and its neighbor Vulcan. These two

## New Guinea and Borneo

erupt simultaneously, because they share the same magmatic chamber. The eruption of Tavurvur in 1937 completely destroyed the town of Rabaul, killing over 500 people. This was followed by several other eruptions, including one in 1994 that caused severe damage to the rebuilt town. Its last eruption occurred in October 2006.

[Left] Puncak Jaya, known as the Carstensz Pyramid, is the highest mountain in Oceania.

[1] to [3] Mount Kinabalu in northeast Borneo harbors some extraordinary plants, particularly the carnivorous Nepentheae.

**3** [1] Landscape in New Guinea.
[2] and [right] The Grasberg mine in Borneo is the world's biggest source of gold and the second biggest source of copper.
[3] Morning view of the Karawen Mountains.

The most inhospitable mountain range in the world is situated in Antarctica. Mount Vinson (16,066 ft./4,897 m) stands close to the South Pole, towering over Mount Tyree (15,896 ft./4,845 m) and Mount Shinn (9,921 ft./3,024 m).

Mount Vinson, part of the Ellesworth Mountains, is surrounded by ten peaks higher than 13,000 ft. (4,000 m). Most of these mountains have never been explored as the way is blocked by enormous ice floes. Mount Vinson itself was only climbed for the first time in 1966, by a roped party of ten Americans. The ascent itself does not present any major technical difficulties, but the access to this mountain and the region's extreme climatic conditions deter most climbers—not to mention the prohibitive cost of such an expedition. The base camp was mounted by a private organization and could only be reached by small plane via Chile. The Erebus volcano (13,205 ft./4,025 m) has been explored more fully and has been regularly scaled by experienced climbers.

Another accessible peak—that of Mount Nansen (13,156 ft./4,010 m), situated between the South Pole and the Ross Sea—is the highest point in the Queen Maud Mountains. Some 75 mi. (120 km) from the South Pole, the Pond volcano (1,778 ft./542 m), on Disappointment Island, in the Sea of Scotland, is active and considered dangerous. Its last eruption, in 1967, caused severe damage to the international scientific stations based in the area.

# Antarctica and Its Glaciers

The Queen Alexandra massif, in the Transantarctic Mountains, culminates with Mount Kirkpatrick (14,856 ft./4,528 m), where a collection of fossils has revealed evidence of the warm climate once enjoyed by this area (referred to as Pangaea in that era). Paleontologists have discovered numerous dinosaur bones here.

[1] and [2] Mountain on Livingston Island.
[3] Glacier Charity, on Livingston Island.

[4] Antarctic volcano covered with ice.
[5] Group of glaciers in Antarctica.

[1] Mount Erebus, on Ross Island, surrounded by ice.
[2] Rocky peaks in Antarctica.
[3] Wright Valley, in the Transantarctica Mountains.

[4] and [5] Smoking crater of the Erebus volcano.
[6] Mountain in Nekkor Harbor.

[1] Gentoo penguins are distinguished by their red beak.
[2] Young Emperor penguins waiting for their parents to return with food.

[4] Mountain on Wiencke
Island.
[5] Climber on the top of the
mountains overlooking
Taylor Valley.
[6] Sunset over Antarctica.

363

# On the Open Sea

**T**he highest mountain in the Caribbean is situated in Jamaica: the Blue Mountains Peak (7,218 ft./2,200 m), best known for its plantations that produce the finest — and most expensive — coffee in the world. The volcanoes of Mount Pelée and La Soufrière, however, have earned a more sinister reputation.

The volcanic activity found in the Caribbean is extremely powerful, as eruptions occur as a result of explosions that emit burning clouds that destroy everything in their path. Even those volcanoes that do not display a high level of activity are capable of awakening very suddenly. The smaller Caribbean islands possess several active volcanoes, such as Mount Carmichael, Le Nez Cassé, L'Échelle, La Citerne, La Madeleine, and, above all, La Soufrière (4,813 ft./1,467 m), nicknamed the "Old Lady," which is situated in Guadeloupe. This volcano does not have a real crater but has several eruptive cones that give off sulfurous steam. Its last eruption occurred in 1976, sparking the evacuation of around 76,000 people — and fierce public debate.

Mount Pelée (4,583 ft./1,397 m) is another famous volcano. Its most significant eruption took place in 1902 and resulted in the total destruction of the town of Saint-Pierre, with 29,000 dead and only two survivors — one a prisoner protected by the walls of his cell, and the other a shoemaker living on the outskirts of the town. Saint-

# Caribbean Mountains

Pierre was completely rebuilt but it has had to withstand other, less devastating, eruptions: one in September 1929, and another in December 1932. The Caribbean has one particularly famous mountain range: the Sierra Maestra, in Cuba, which provided shelter for Che Guevara and Fidel Castro. Its highest peak is Turquino (6,476 ft./1,974 m).

[1] The village of Morne-Rouge, in Martinica, overshadowed by Mount Pelée.
[2] Mount Pelée climbs to a height of 4,583 ft. (1,397 m).

[Opposite page] Saint-Pierre, at the foot of Mount Pelée, was rebuilt after being completely destroyed by the volcano.

[1] A palm grove on the slopes of Turquino in Cuba.
[2] A hill in Cuba.
[3] Rocky peaks in the Viñales Valley in Cuba.

Caribbean Mountains

[4] to [6] Los Ingenios
Mountains and Valley, Cuba.

[1] Hikers in a canyon bordered by the volcanoes of the Valley of Desolation, in Dominica.
[2] Lake Boeri, in Dominica.
[3] Hot water lake, in Dominica.
[4] Coconuts and extinct volcanoes, Dominica.

[5] Thick palm forest in Dominica.
[6] and [7] Mountain range in the National Park of the Dominican Republic, with the Pico Duarte (10,128 ft./3,087 m), the highest mountain in the Caribbean.

[1] and [2] The various peaks of La Soufrière (4,813 ft./1,467 m), a volcano in Guadeloupe.

**5** [3] to [5] La Soufrière's eruptions of lava end up in the sea, where they cool and thus extend the island's surface area.

375

[1] to [4] La Soufrière's name is derived from the high sulfur content of its gas emissions.

[5] The town of Sainte-Lucie is often shrouded in a yellowish fog laden with sulfur from La Soufrière. [6] and [7] The crater contains pure sulfur, while the gas emissions mainly consist of sulfur dioxide, which has a strong smell of rotten eggs.

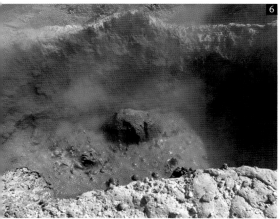

[Opposite page] A town in Trinidad.

[1] A village in the Viñales Valley in Cuba.
[2] A village at the foot of the Escambray Mountains in Cuba.

The American state of Hawaii comprises a chain of 122 islands. The main ones are Niihau, Kauai, Oahu, Molokai, Lanai, Kahoolawe, and, of course, the island of Hawaii itself. They are situated in an area where the earth's crust gives rise to active volcanoes that are extinguished when their mass of magma moves.

The main volcanoes in Hawaii are Hualalai (8,271 ft./2,521 m) and Kilauea (4,009 ft./1,222 m), considered among the most active volcanoes in the world, along with Etna, Stromboli, and the Piton de la Fournaise. Kilauea has spewed out millions of cubic meters of lava every year since 1983. This lava runs down to the ocean and is called "Pele's hair," as it is smooth and shiny. Although this volcano is highly active, it is not particularly dangerous, as it is not explosive. Mauna Kea would be considered the highest mountain in the world (at 33,563 ft./10,230 m) if its underwater section was taken into account; its visible part measures 13,796 ft./4,205 m. Mauna Kea, which means "White Mountain," is a dormant volcano; several telescopes have been installed on its ice-capped peak, as its air is exceptionally pure. It is a sacred site for Hawaiians. Another holy mountain, Mauna Loa (23,681 ft./4,170 m), is the second highest mountain in Hawaii. It is an active volcano with regular eruptions (generally every five years). Mauna Loa is closely monitored, as its eruptions could affect inhabited areas. It displayed little activity until 2002, but since then its magma has risen and earthquakes have occurred

# The Islands of Hawaii

around the volcano—both signs of an imminent and violent eruption that could knock down its walls and trigger a devastating tsunami, like the ones with 1,000-ft. (300-m)-high waves that devastated the region 100,000 years ago.

[1] and [2] Puuo Oo, one of the craters of Kilauea, ejecting lava.
[3] and [4] Caldera of the Kilauea volcano.

[5] to [7] The lava from Kilauea runs toward the sea; it is known as "Pele's hair."

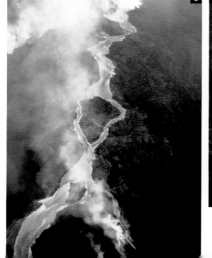

[1] and [3] Mauna Kea is a holy mountain for Hawaiians, who call it the "White Mountain." [2] A radio telescope has been installed on the top of Mauna Kea.

[4] Mauna Loa is a dormant volcano but it is considered dangerous.
[5] and [6] Mauna Kea is the highest peak in Hawaii. If its underwater part is taken into account, it stands as the world's highest mountain (33,563 ft./10,230 m).

The Gulf of Lanzarote,
on the Canary Island
of the same name.

The Canary Islands, situated off the shores of Morocco, comprise seven main islands: Lanzarote, Fuerteventura, Gran Canaria, Tenerife, La Gomera, La Palma, and El Hierro. These islands are distinguished by significant volcanic activity, particularly apparent on Mount Teide (12,188 ft./3,715 m).

The name Teide means "hell" in the ancestral language of Tenerife. Traditionally it was a taboo mountain that could not be climbed (for fear of death). Climbers from the European mainland were undeterred, however, and Sir Edmund Scory scaled it for the first time in 1582. Nowadays a cable car takes tourists up to a height of 11,663 ft. (3,555 m) before they tackle the final stretch on foot, right up to the smoking, sulfurous crater, 230 ft. (70 m) in diameter and 148 ft. (45 m) deep. The last eruption of Mount Teide took place in 1909, and it has been dormant ever since. It is surrounded by other volcanoes, such as El Pico Viejo (10,282 ft./3,134 m).

The island of Lanzarote is set in the Timanfaya National Park, which protects the twenty-five low craters of the "Mountains of Fire." Another park, Los Volcanes, also contains volcanoes, along with numerous paleolithic fossils. Gran Canaria has at its center El Pico de las Nieves (6,394 ft./1,949 m), with a beautiful wood of endemic Canary Pines at its foot.

As a whole, this group of islands harbors extraordinary plant life, particularly the fa-

# The Canary Islands

mous dragon trees on Tenerife, which date back over 3,000 years. They ooze a red resin believed to have magical and therapeutic powers. The cooled lava at the foot of the volcanoes on Lanzarote is ideally suited to the cultivation of vines, each of which is surrounded by a small stone wall to protect it from strong winds.

[Left] and [1] Chain of volcanoes on Lanzarote.

[2] A caravan of dromedaries in the Timanfaya National Park, in Lanzarote.
[3] Vegaipala, on the island of Lanzarote.

389

[1 to 3] The Roque Bentaiga (4,632 ft/1,412 m) on the island of Gran Canaria.

[4] The Valley of La Laguna, seen from Mount Teide on Tenerife.
[5] The peak of Mount Teide.
[6] Las Canadas National Park, on Tenerife.

Aerial view of the Piton
de la Fournaise and
the Bellecombe Pass.

This island close to Mauritius and Madagascar was created two million years after the emergence of an underwater volcano, the Piton des Neiges (10,072 ft./3,070 m). This volcano has been dormant for 12,000 years—unlike the Piton de la Fournaise (8,632 ft./2,631 m), which is considered one of the most active volcanoes in the world.

The Piton de la Fournaise, situated in the southeast of the island, comprises a large dome in the middle of a "U" around 8 mi. (13 km) long, known as the Enclosure. The volcano has two craters—Bory, to the west, and Dolomieu, to the east. The latter appeared in 1791 in the wake of a terrible eruption that triggered the collapse of a magma chamber (a large cavity 6–30 mi. (10–50 km) below ground level containing molten rock). When the magma rose to the surface, it gave rise to explosive eruptions. Alongside the Enclosure stands the Piton de Crac (4,488 feet/1,368 m), another vestige of previous eruptions. The configuration of the Piton de la Fournaise has changed constantly as a result of its various eruptions. It is a young volcano, less than 5,000 years old, hence its volatility. Its sides crack regularly to reveal gushing lava that concentrates on a single point before being propelled into the air. When it falls, it hurtles down the slopes of the mountain. Once the lava has cooled, it forms protruding cones, or "pitons."

# Réunion Island

Although the Piton de la Fournaise erupts frequently, it can also sleep for periods of several years. Its most devastating eruptions took place in 1860 and, more recently, in 1961, when it spewed out smoke to a height of 20,000 ft. (6,000 m). Another eruption in 1986 left a hollow more than 490 ft. (150 m) deep in the Dolomieu crater.

[1] The Piton de la Fournaise
[2 to 4] Tourists walking along a path that has been created for observing the crater of the Piton de la Fournaise.

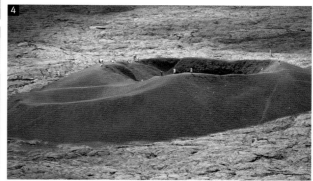

[5] The Cirque de Mafate, with the Piton des Neiges in the background.
[6] The Rivière des Remparts, with the Piton des Neiges to the rear.

[Opposite page] and [1]
The Cirque de Cilaos.

[2] and [3] The post in the
isolated villages in the center
of Réunion is delivered on foot.

[1] Waterfall on the Cirque de Mafate.
[2] The Cirque de Salazie.
[3] A mountain lake.

[4] Waterfalls in the Grande Ravine, in Saint-Joseph.
[5] and [6] The Trou de Fer, on the Cirque de Mafate.
[7] One of Réunion's pedestrian postmen.

Tahiti is the biggest island in French Polynesia, and its surface of 400 sq. mi. (1,045 km²) is marked by several volcanoes. Mount Orohena (7,352 ft./2,241 m) is the highest, followed by Pito Iti (6,923 ft./2,110 m) and Mount Aorai (6,778 ft./2,066 m).

There are two types of Polynesian island: high ones that emerged from underwater volcanoes and lower ones and atolls that resulted from the collapse of volcanoes. None of the Polynesian volcanoes are active any more. Tahiti is divided into two parts: the large island, or Tahiti Nui, and the peninsula jutting out to the southeast, the small island, or Tahiti Iti. It forms part of the Society Islands, and more precisely the subgroup of the Windward Islands. The highest mountains are found on Tahiti Nui, where the interior of the island comprises a huge crater surrounded by high peaks. Alongside the three highest of these peaks stand the rugged Diadem (4,334 ft./1,321 m) and Mount Marau (4,898 ft./1,493 m), neither of which is difficult to climb. The Tahiti Iti peninsula contains Mount Ronui (4,370 ft./1,332 m), endowed with stunning escarpments.

Bora Bora, Maupiti, Raiatea, and Tahaa are components of the Society Islands known collectively as the Leeward Islands. The smallest, Maupiti (4 sq. mi./11 km²), is a volcano, Teura Faatui (1,220 ft./372 m), also known as Mount Nuupure, set within a transparent lagoon bounded by a coral reef. Bora

# The Polynesian Islands

Bora, the site of Mount Otemanu (2,305 ft./727 m), is similarly encircled by a coral reef.

French Polynesia is completed by the Tuamotu, Gambier, Austral, and Marquesas Islands. The latter archipelago is the youngest, geologically speaking; the mountains are steep and barely eroded, while the shorelines are devoid of coral reefs.

[1] The island of Hiva Oa, in French Polynesia.
[2] Pleasure boats anchored in the Bay of Virgins.

[3] A coral reef surrounds Moorea, an island close to Tahiti.
[4] and [5] The turquoise sea of Bora Bora under the shadow of an extinct volcano.

[1] Volcanic island of Moorea.
[2] Mount Mouaroa 2,887 ft. (880 m), on the island of Moorea.
[3] Growing pineapples on the island of Moorea.

[4] and [5] Rocky crags
on Mount Mouaroa.
[6] Horses on the slopes
of Mouaroa.

[Following pages]
Road running through the
mountains of Samoa.

**T**he volcanoes of Vanuatu lie to the north of New Caledonia, in an area where the Australian and Pacific plates converge. They belong to the Pacific Ring of Fire, which concentrates almost 70 per cent of the world's volcanic activity.

These volcanoes, distinguished by viscous and explosive magma mixed with water, produce hydro-magmatic explosions of very great force. Some of the Vanuatu volcanoes display constant activity, particularly those on the islands of Tanna and Ambrym; others have been dormant for decades but are capable of awakening and emitting gas. A number of these volcanoes are subterranean and their eruptions give rise to new islands. When the process begins, the sea first turns a yellow-gray color; this is followed by the emergence of a mass of rocks in a cloud of smoke and ashes, accompanied by a deafening noise. The island of Karua was born in this way. The volcano came to the surface in 1948, creating an island around 1 mi. (1.5 km) in diameter and 330 ft. (100 m) in altitude. It disappeared in the 1950s, only to re-emerge in 1975.

The island of Ambrym is occupied by two active volcanoes: Benbow (3,806 ft./1,160 m) and Marum (4,167 ft./1,270 m). The latter has three craters, the biggest of which groans loudly, earning it the nickname of the Wild Pig. The island of Gaua, to the northeast of Vanuatu, possesses the most dangerous volcano in the region: Mount Garet,

# The Volcanoes of Vanuatu

with merely 2,625 ft. (800 m) above sea level but a submerged section over 6,562 ft. (2,000 m) deep. This volcano appeared to be extinct until 1962, but in 1973 violent earth tremors shook the region; an ejection of ash followed in January 1974, indicating a rise in the magma levels. Since then its activity has only intensified, and experts fear the worst.

[1] to [3] The Yasur volcano is situated on the island of Tanna. It is still active.

[4] and [5] The Yasur volcano spews out ash, volcanic bombs, and acid rain that destroy the surrounding vegetation.

411

**3** [1] to [3] The bay surrounding the Yasur volcano has an abundance of fish, as its waters are heated by the subterranean magma.

[4] to [6] The inhabitants of the island of Tanna supplicate the Yasur volcano with ceremonial dances. This community's life is now being disrupted by the arrival of tour operators.

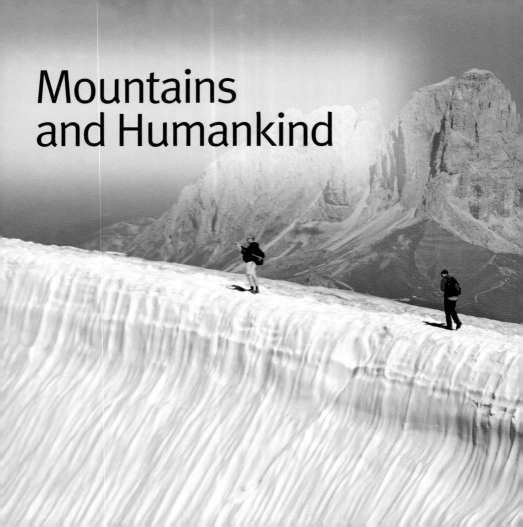

# Mountains
# and Humankind

O n May 29, 1953, Edmund Hillary and the sherpa Tenzing Norgay reached the peak of Mount Everest. This remarkable achievement earned the New Zealander a knighthood and admission to the Order of the Garter.

Sir Edmund Hillary went on to climb other Himalayan peaks before dedicating his life to the defense of the peoples of Nepal. He died on January 11, 2008. Many other climbers have followed in his footsteps up Everest. Twenty-five made it to the top in 1978, 146 in 2000, and over 500 in 2007. Once the highest peak had been conquered, however, climbers sought new challenges, the most daunting being the ascent of all the fourteen mountains higher than 26,000 ft. (8,000 m).

A mere fifteen climbers have accomplished this feat, starting with the Italian Reinhold Messner, who climbed these fourteen peaks between 1970 and 1986. He was followed by the Pole Jerzy Kukuczka, the Swiss Erhard Loretan, the Mexican Carlos Carsolio, the Pole Krystof Wielicki, the Spaniard Juanito Oiarzabal, and the Italian Sergio Martini. The first woman to climb Everest was the Japanese Junko Tabei, in 1975.

The Himalayas now play host to countless expeditions, many of them ignoring the most basic safety requirements. It is important not to allow the achievements of a few experienced climbers to obscure the extreme danger lurking on these slopes: over 300 climbers have lost their lives on the fourteen mountains rising above 26,000 ft. (8,000 m). As for the roof of Europe, Mont Blanc, this was first conquered on August 7, 1786, by Frenchmen Michel Gabriel Paccard and Jacques Balmat.

# Great Climbers

[1] Sir Edmund Hillary, the first climber to reach the top of Everest.
[2] Sir Chris Bonington was the first to climb the south face of Annapurna and he has taken part in nine Himalayan expeditions.
[3] Ed Viesturs was the first American to climb all the fourteen peaks higher than 26,000 (8,000 m).
[4] Sir Edmund Hillary and the Sherpa Tenzing Norgay on their triumphal return to London.

[5] British expedition to the peak of Kongur, in China.
[6] This German-Austrian team was the first to climb the Himalayan mountain of Nanga Prabat, since been dubbed the "German Mountain."

419

[1] Jean-Marc Boivin on the slopes of Aconcagua in Argentina.
[2] Maurice Herzog, who successfully climbed Annapurna.
[3] Junko Tabei, the first woman to reach the top of Everest.

[4] to [7] Catherine Destivelle was considered the world's best female climber between 1985 and 1988.

**A**s well as serious climbing, mountains offer the possibility of numerous sport and leisure activities—not only skiing but also snowboarding, dogsled racing, rock climbing, trekking, mountain biking, paragliding, and snowshoeing.

Skiing has developed enormously in the last few years, aided by new materials and disciplines like off-trail skiing and snowboarding. One of the most spectacular formats is extreme skiing, which involves hurtling down steep slopes. Cross-country skiing is a less hair-raising affair that allows its practitioners to travel through mountains without too much difficulty. Snowshoeing provides another means of exploring mountains in winter, while the more technically demanding ski touring consists of walking up a mountain with snowshoes or short skis and then skiing back down.

In fine weather, activities such as mountain biking and aerial sports like paragliding become feasible options, while marked footpaths cater to hikers.

Winter sports competitors have a myriad of events to choose from: downhill skiing, slalom, giant slalom, super-G, combined Apline and Nordic skiing, ski jumping, bobsledding, sledding, skating, surf skiing, half pipe (acrobatic ski surfing), parallel giant slalom (with two skiers racing each other

# Sports and Leisure in the Mountains

simultaneously down two parallel courses), ice hockey, the biathlon (skiing plus rifle shooting), and curling. The latter is a little-known sport, similar to bowling, played on ice by two teams of four people. The aim is to slide stones (fitted with a handle) as close as possible to a target drawn on the ice.

[1] Ski jumping off an escarpment.
[2] and [3] Snowshoeing.

[4] and [5] Cross-country skiing.
[6] A skiing race in the Dolomites.

[1] Hiking in the mountains.
[2] Camping in the high mountains.
[3] Walking in the mountains.

[4] Hikers amidst spectacular mountain scenery.
[5] Donkey rides allow children to explore the Cirque de Gavarnie.

427

[1] to [3] Mountain bikes make it possible to travel virtually anywhere in the mountains.

[4] to [6] It is essential to wear a helmet for mountain biking.

[Following pages]
A couple cycling on the top of the Slickrock Bike Trail in Moab, Utah.

[Left] Inflatable dinghies on a lake in Alaska.

[1] to [3] Riding the rapids in a raft.

**M**ountains provide many professional opportunities for forest rangers, shepherds and guides, while tourism offers a further range of jobs for skiing instructors, equipment rental firms, hoteliers, restaurateurs, and mountain rescue services.

In days gone by, sheep-rearing was the dominant occupation in the mountains, as the flocks fed on the grass on their upper slopes. Nowadays, however, shepherds find it increasingly hard to earn a living. The reintroduction of predatory animals has hardly improved their situation, sparking an ongoing debate about the advantages of maintaining an untouched natural environment versus the merits of a more domesticated, pastoral landscape. The reintroduction of the wolf and the bear has been particularly controversial in this respect.

Shepherds are increasingly finding work related to tourism during the wintertime, operating ski lifts and maintaining ski runs, or working in rural refuges and hotels. Some even offer their services as skiing instructors. Another employment option in the mountains is with the rescue services, from police units to fire brigades. The most prestigious job, however, is that of the mountain guide. Entering this profession involves passing several exams and completing over fifty-five expeditions and climbs. A guide's

## Working in the Mountains

diploma is granted only after five years of study and training.

Other jobs are more specific to particular types of mountains: volcanoes, for example, obviously attract volcanologists, and glaciers glaciologists. Both have made enormous contributions to our understanding of the earth's climate in the distant past.

[1] Overseeing livestock in the Wakhan Corridor, in Afghanistan.
[2] An Indian shepherd in the foothills of the Himalayas.

[3] Livestock is driven up to the high mountain prairies every summer.
[4] This shepherd and his dog are watching over a flock of sheep grazing on the slopes of Mount Iraty, in the Basque Country.
[5] Farmers in the Gullin region of China use buffalo to plow their fields.

[1] A Basque shepherd.
[2] A Peruvian peasant plowing land to plant potatoes, on the slopes of the Andes.
[3] The high mountain valleys of Pakistan are used to grow grain.

**6** [4] to [6] The profession of mountain guide has flourished as a result of the boom in tourism and the growing attraction of climbs up the world's highest mountains.

Mountains claim the lives of hundreds of people every year, many of them victims of their own recklessness. Nature can turn hostile very quickly at high altitudes and a carefree walk can become a nightmare in a sudden snap of bad weather.

Storms often descend very quickly on a mountain. Wind, cold, snow, and fog can often combine to create difficult conditions. Lightning can be extremely fearsome, but sunlight is equally dangerous, as the higher the altitude, the greater the degree of ultraviolet radiation. Sunstroke on a mountain is more serious than the equivalent on a beach. It is vital to wear sunglasses when climbing snowy slopes.

High altitudes can also harbor traps in winter in the form of crevasses hidden in glaciers and, above all, natural avalanches triggered by warm air or off-trail skiers. There are three types of avalanche: those caused by a recent snowfall, those caused by the formation of ice, and those caused by brighter weather in the springtime. Rocks can also be a source of danger. Every mountain has its own geological configuration, but this is not necessarily stable, and landslides generally occur without any prior warning. Altitude itself causes numerous accidents. The higher one climbs, the thinner the oxygen, making physical exertion

# The Danger of Mountains

more difficult. Furthermore, the temperature drops by 33°F (1°C) for every 328 ft. (100 m) climbed. The wind also increases in speed and the sun's rays become stronger. These circumstances can combine to cause hypoxia, accompanied by headache, nausea, vertigo, breathlessness, and severe fatigue. These symptoms are indicators of a condition known as altitude sickness.

440

[1] and [2] Ski resorts put up signs to warn of dangers, but this does not prevent careless visitors from ignoring their recommendations and prohibitions.
[3] Very high peaks such as Everest are subject to frequent blizzards that severely impair visibility.

**5** [4] An avalanche in the Pakistani Himalayas has just caught this group of climbers by surprise.
[5] Roped climbers try to advance in a blizzard.

[1] to [3] Fractures are among the most frequent injuries to climbers. Victims are carried in a resin or aluminum stretcher to a point where a helicopter can pick them up and take them to the nearest hospital.

The Dangers of Mountains

[4] Rain is often accompanied by violent storms in the mountains. [5] Lightning is common in the mountains, particularly in passes between two peaks.

445

N ew materials, mass tourism, deforestation, and the exploitation of natural resources through mining, agriculture, and hunting have a significant impact on the environment of a mountain range. In order to curb these effects, a number of natural parks have been created to protect mountainous areas.

Such measures do not, however, entirely prevent pollution caused by human hand. The slopes of Everest have become a veritable garbage dump, and elsewhere hiking trails and mountain footpaths are littered with cans and other debris. Moreover, noise and trash disrupt the lifestyle of animals, while the untimely picking of flowers and the trampling underfoot of the land has led to the eradication of numerous plant species, such as the famous Lady's Slipper, a particularly beautiful orchid.

Most mountain plants and animals are not easy to relocate and acclimatize poorly to lower altitudes. These plants are protected species that cannot be picked under any circumstances, and it is similarly forbidden to catch or feed endangered animal species. Global warming caused by human activity has occasioned major changes in mountains (the melting of glaciers, for example). It is therefore essential to limit the emissions of carbon dioxide if we want to continue marveling at snow-capped peaks and ski down their slopes without the assistance of snow machines. It is also necessary to restrict infrastructures that disrupt the environment under the pretext of providing tourists with

# Protecting Mountains

less arduous ways of admiring high peaks or smoking craters. These can take the form of cable cars leading to the edge of a crater, landing strips offering a short cut to a Himalayan peak, or roads that allow buses to deposit tourists close to a mountain top.

[1] The mountains of Irian Jaya are slashed by deep fissures, as they conceal vast reserves of oil and copper.
[2] A copper mine.

[Opposite page] Mountain flowers in the Dolomites.

[1] Fields of wild mustard in the Torres de la Paine National Park in Chile.
[2] Wild flowers near Sesto, in the Dolomites.
[3] Despite its appearance, the bear grass in the Montana Glacier National Park in fact belongs to the lily family.

[4] Hiking through the Fiscalino Pass, in the Dolomites.
[5] Path leading to the foot of Lavaredo, in the Dolomites.

[1] Cable car in Valais in the Swiss Alps.
[2] Cable car in the Zugspitze in the Bavarian Alps.
[3] Hotel terrace in a ski resort.
[4] Great swathes of forest were removed from this mountain in British Columbia to allow skiers to indulge in their hobby.
[5] Snow cannons can be activated at night to ensure that the ski runs can be used the next day.

453

# Index

*Acknowledgements:*
*To my father Lucien Viard, a climber and great lover of the Alps*

**Photo Credits**
**All the photographs in this book belong to the Corbis agency.**